Talking Sense in Science

Talking Sense in Science is a highly practical guide to getting the most out of primary science lessons through talking with children. This clearly written and straightforward book helps teachers to support understanding by developing their own interaction in the classroom. Each idea is described and illustrated and followed by a short task to develop teaching skills. Key topics covered are:

- ways of understanding in science, and scientific language
- how talk can support practical activities
- developing understanding through a science conversation
- what to say, when to say it and how to say it.

Examples given in the book span the range of primary school science topics, and provide an ideal sourcebook of lesson ideas. *Talking Sense in Science* is an essential buy for primary teachers who want an accessible way to improve their practice and their pupils' understanding in science. It is also an ideal learning tool for student teachers.

Douglas P. Newton is a Professor of Education at Newcastle University. He has researched and published widely in the fields of science education and supporting understanding.

Talking Sense in Science

Helping children understand
through talk

Douglas P. Newton

London and New York

First published 2002
by RoutledgeFalmer
11 New Fetter Lane, London EC4P 4EE

Simultaneously published in the USA and Canada
by Routledge
29 West 35th Street, New York, NY 10001

RoutledgeFalmer is an imprint of the Taylor & Francis Group

Typeset in Bembo by
Keystroke, Jacaranda Lodge, Wolverhampton
Printed and bound in Great Britain by
Biddles Ltd, Guildford and King's Lynn

British Library Cataloguing in Publication Data
A catalogue record for this book is available
from the British Library

Library of Congress Cataloging in Publication Data
Newton, Douglas P.
    Talking sense in science: helping children understand
    through talk / Douglas P. Newton.
        p. cm.
    Includes bibliographical references and index.
    ISBN 0–415–25351–9
    1. Science – study and teaching (Elementary) 2. Communication
    in education. I. Title.

LB 1585. N44 2002
372. 3'5044—dc21   2001031913

ISBN 0–415–25351–9

Contents

Illustrations

Figures

Table

Introduction

In primary or elementary school classrooms you will find children busy doing science. They listen to the teacher, do some practical work, complete a worksheet, respond in a quiz and do many of the other mundane activities we associate with classroom life. But sometimes, science is done but never thought about, acquired but never really understood, isolated from what children already know and soon forgotten. There may be nothing wrong with the activities themselves but, nevertheless, learning is superficial. This book is about getting more out of science lessons, improving the quality of children's learning and developing habits of thought that will serve children well in the future. It is not about throwing out your cherished teaching activities and starting again; it is about making the most of them. This is done largely through talk, through what you and the children have to say to one another. The book illustrates and practises the use of talk to support children's understanding in science. Step by step, it takes you through what understanding means in science, how to help children build an understanding, strategies that will help you foster understanding, and how you can help make new understandings secure.

Talk is a powerful way of supporting understanding in science. By talk, I do not mean simply telling children things, although there will be times when that could be the right thing to do. Talk includes, for example, setting the scene, eliciting what children already know or believe, asking for a prediction, obliging children to explain, making suggestions, monitoring learning and, in bigger chunks, having a conversation. It also means being, at times, non-committal, declaring puzzlement or doubt, wondering why, and expressing enthusiasm and astonishment. All this talk, however, is not gossip. Its purpose is to help the children make sense of their thoughts. It helps you – and the children – make the most of the investment of time and effort you and they give to the lesson.

Understanding is a powerful kind of knowing. An understanding of science adds to your ability to cope in the world. You are less likely to be exploited and more likely to deal with new problems successfully and flexibly. At the same time, it can satisfy a natural curiosity and give you a way of relating to the world. These benefits are more likely to accrue if we make understanding a central concern for ourselves and for the children. This is not to say that facts and figures are unimportant. For instance, it is obviously important to know that lightning can kill and that, in an open space, it tends to strike trees more often than the flat fields they stand in. The scientist, however, wants to know why lightning can kill and why it tends to strike the trees more often than the flat field. In other words, as in other subjects, reasons matter.

Some see understanding as a finite achievement: you either understand something or you do not. If you do, then it is time to move on to the next item and add that trophy to the collection – a 'seen it, done it' approach. But, even when we grasp something, our grasp may be tenuous, limited or partial. Some things will not sit comfortably with other things we know and we suppress disturbing questions that keep coming to the surface. When they do come to the surface we may feel that expressing them attracts unwelcome attention and risks making us look foolish. We find that our understanding works well in one context but not in another. Our new-born understanding is not yet as coherent, organized and integrated with our existing knowledge as it might be. This can take time and needs opportunities for children to express their thoughts. Talk can do that and can reveal the disturbing questions and discontinuities in their understandings. In the process, the children have to express and address them in order to maintain their end of the discussion. Often, they will be successful but, if they are not, you are aware of it and can shape the talk to help the child.

Seeing the dawn of an understanding can be very gratifying. It can, of course, be started by a variety of things. Direct experience, for instance, leaves powerful traces in the mind and, quite correctly, we try to provide children with as much of it as we can. Merely providing experience, however, is not always enough. Experience can be narrow, restricted, partial, confusing, chaotic and overwhelming. Events can even pass unnoticed. Direct, first-hand experience is a very useful way of developing skills and supporting learning. It can provide an important foundation for understanding. It does not, however, come with a guarantee that it will produce an acceptable understanding, or any understanding at all. No activity can offer such a guarantee and we cannot expect children to make sense of everything unaided. They often need guidance that helps them make the most of their experience and increases the likelihood that reasonable and well-founded understandings result. Talking with children is a way of guiding thoughts and providing opportunities for expressing and exploring such understandings as they develop. Talk can gently guide attention, give direction and develop new perspectives when things begin to go wrong, or go nowhere at all. It allows a child to engage in the experience, even go down false paths but, in the end, it ensures that thinking is productive and checks that it is sound.

In some subjects, talk is relatively easy to initiate and maintain. The language is generally easy to grasp and the topic relates readily to experience. The way science is expressed is not always so user friendly, everyday experience and 'common sense' can be misleading and not every teacher is a scientist. When teachers feel less confident, they may talk less about what matters most so understanding suffers. Even those with a background in science may not make the most of what they – and the children – do. They may keep the children attentive or busy but attention and activity do not come with a guarantee that understanding will follow. For example, young children will probably pay close attention while you pull out 'body organs' from a stuffed figure, naming the parts as you do so. Nevertheless, their understanding of a topic on *Ourselves* could be very odd unless you had a lot more to say. You do not, for instance, have direct access to kidneys through your mouth but the stuffed toy's anatomy suggests that you do. Similarly, children exploring what makes things float will probably be asked to test a variety of objects in water. They may seek no pattern, expect no pattern, notice no pattern, even jump to a partial pattern early and persist with it. Children are, after all, only human. They may not be as systematic as you would be and, if they are, they may not notice what matters among all the things that could matter (such as colour, size, shape, solidity and density). Having come to a conclusion that works some of the time, they may ignore those occasions when it does not work (for example, the object that sinks, in spite of being hollow) unless you have something to say. Even though you may not be a scientist, what you say can make a difference. What it takes is forethought and a readiness to explore ideas together.

You cannot give people an understanding, they must work at it themselves. But people are different and they work at understanding in different ways. You, on the other hand, will have your own, preferred ways of teaching. You feel comfortable with them and feel you perform well using them. But some children may not get the most out of the way you work so, at times, you have to be prepared to do things in other ways.

Some children may be timid or prefer to avoid the risk of failure by keeping quiet and you may have to arrange opportunities that draw them out without reinforcing a fear of failure. This means that science talk, like any other talk, needs to be considerate and allow for variation in children. What works well with one child may not work well with another. Thinking and feeling are not as separate as we often treat them. Children should want to talk science and that means it should be rewarding for them. Often, curiosity, the desire for competence, knowledge about themselves, the world and how they relate to it is sufficient. Showing some enthusiasm yourself helps as it is catching and shows that you value what learning science has to offer. The children must also expect some success. Here, success is defined in terms of understanding so children need to know that it is among the achievements that count.

When governments and their agents give their exclusive attention to one or two areas of learning, it is easy for others to lose their way. For instance, a concern for literacy and numeracy is both reasonable and desirable and lessons in science might make a useful contribution. But we must remember that this is *not* the only reason or even the main reason for teaching science. Science is not taught simply to service other subjects. We teach it because of the understandings and insights it gives us.

The book is divided into four parts. Part 1, *Understanding and science: why and what*, is about what understanding means in the context of science. It also discusses some aspects of the language of science and illustrates how to make it meaningful. In any subject, constructing an understanding is not always easy and it helps if you have a clear view of where you want to go. Part 2, *Helping children understand: guiding thought*, describes how to help children construct understandings in a topic through dialogue. It begins with how to prepare the way and lay foundations and goes on to the development of an acceptable understanding in your target topic. Practical activity can support understanding in science if used properly so how you might make the most of it is discussed and illustrated. There are other things you can do to help that will support your teaching and some of these are described in Part 3, *Doing more for understanding*. This is, of course, an important step but it is only a first step. Initial understandings can be tenuous and short-lived. Part 4, *Conversations in science*, describes ways of improving the quality of those understandings. The word 'conversation' was chosen because it is a reminder that the focus is on providing opportunities for children to discuss their science at greater length and in greater depth.

The progression in the book is from helping children build or change an understanding to developing it, integrating it, and making it better.

The examples illustrate episodes in science lessons. For them to make sense (and to be practically useful), they often include talk which goes beyond the immediate aim of the section in hand. Thus, for instance, talk that supports practical activity and the role of prediction are discussed in sections of their own. Practical activity and prediction have not, however, been expunged from the examples of classroom practice before and after those sections. To do so would make them unrealistic and would limit their usefulness. In effect, various aspects of talk are highlighted in turn but their wider contexts give them meaning and practical utility.

This is a practical book that aims to show ways of using science talk to help a child construct an understanding and make it sound. In essence, it is a self-help book for all who must teach science in the primary or elementary school. The emphasis is on developing your skills quickly in contexts that have immediate classroom application. There are many examples that illustrate what talk can do. You could treat these examples as a resource and adapt and try them in the classroom. There are also activities in the book that you can use to develop and practise your expertise. Please try them as you go along. Most of the time, what you produce will be of use in your science lessons. There is a variety of feasible responses to these activities and yours is likely to reflect the circumstances you teach in. Nevertheless, some possibilities are suggested in the 'Endnote' but, inevitably, the suggestions cannot be exhaustive. Just because your idea is not included does not necessarily mean that it is 'wrong'. Those that are described will let you know if your thinking is, at least, of the right kind. In any event, the final test of what is 'right' is in the classroom, so test your ideas there and refine them afterwards.

Your science lessons

Before you begin, you might like to spend a minute or two thinking about what you focus on in your science lessons. What is the flavour of your science teaching? Think through a recent lesson. Here are a few questions to help you. Put a tick in the boxes that most reflect your lesson (+ means very much like your lesson, − means not very much like your lesson). These are just a few of the possible questions that could be asked about the quality of a science lesson. You may want to add others yourself.

	+	−
Do you tie the science firmly to the children's own experience?	☐☐☐☐☐	
Do you focus on understanding rather than learning facts?	☐☐☐☐☐	
Do you say things that help them make key mental connections?	☐☐☐☐☐	
Do you ask for significant explanations and reasons?	☐☐☐☐☐	
Do the children think in depth and at length about their science?	☐☐☐☐☐	
Do you consistently press children to justify their responses?	☐☐☐☐☐	
Do you have the children talk at length about their science?	☐☐☐☐☐	
Do you feel you make the most of your teaching resources?	☐☐☐☐☐	
Do you show enthusiasm?	☐☐☐☐☐	
Do the children show interest?	☐☐☐☐☐	
Are you happy with the *quality* of learning?	☐☐☐☐☐	

Part 1

Understanding and science: why and what

The aim is to help children understand their science. You cannot give them an understanding. Ultimately, they must construct it for themselves but you can do a lot to help that process. In the child's mind, understandings could range from superficial and fragile to profound and secure. To begin with, a child's understanding may be limited, even tentative, and it may not sit comfortably with what the child already knows. Such an understanding needs to be nurtured if it is to survive. It helps if you have a fairly clear idea of the kind of understanding you want. Of course, a clear target is not enough. You always have to make what you say meaningful, otherwise you do not make contact with the children's thinking. In this part of the book, the nature of some understandings in science is illustrated and what makes them worthwhile is discussed. It concludes with some thoughts about the language of science and how it can be made meaningful for the children.

1.1 WHY UNDERSTAND?

Constructing an understanding for yourself or helping someone to understand can take a lot of mental effort. Is it worth it? Compare Maurice Memorizer and Marvin Makesense. Maurice spends his time memorizing as much as he can. Marvin tries to makes sense of it. As a result, Marvin is not always as quick as Maurice when it comes to giving answers but Maurice generally comes unstuck when he meets something new. For example, there was a torch that would not work. Maurice remembered that he had seen people change the bulb when that happened. He tried it but the torch still did not work. 'No problem', he thought, 'I've also seen people change the battery to make a torch work'. He tried that, too, but it still did not work. All he could do now was poke around at random and hope something would happen. 'I don't really know what I'm doing', he thought.

Marvin understood electricity so he had a try. 'For the bulb to work, we need a complete circuit for the electricity to flow around. As the battery and bulb are new, it's more likely that there is a break in the circuit.' He followed the path that the electricity would have to take from the top of the battery, through the bulb, through the switch and to the bottom of the battery. At the bottom of the battery was a spring that the electricity had to pass through. The old battery had left a white deposit on it. 'That's it!' he thought, scraping it off. 'That's what is breaking the circuit.' The circuit was now complete, the bulb lit, the problem was solved, and it was understanding that did it.

Here, understanding helped Marvin deal with something he had not met before. Unlike Maurice's memorized knowledge, Marvin's knowledge is flexible and can be applied in new situations. More than that, understanding supports further learning and is a durable kind of knowledge. Think of the early understanding of money that people develop when they are quite young. It lasts a lifetime and underpins their greater understanding of money matters that they develop sub-sequently. In the same way, I still remember my first understanding of the reflection of light from a flat mirror. The teacher made an analogy with a ball bouncing off a wall and this helped me grasp what happened to the light rays. Much later, I found it helped me grasp explanations of how curved reflectors, like spoons, produce their peculiar images. An understanding can also help people resist manipulation and exploitation. With it, it is more difficult for others to take advantage or act against our best interests. Similarly, a grasp of ways of working in science can help us evaluate claims about the testing of a variety of products from soap powders to genetically modified crops. But, not everything that is worth understanding is of immediate, practical use. If the reason for understanding rested only on that, a lot of what we teach – even in science – would have no place. Knowing about space, the planets and the stars, for instance, probably has little practical utility for most people. Nevertheless, they often want to understand such things. Having an understanding of our place in the world (the universe in this case) and knowing why things are as we see them satisfies a psychological need. Children show this need in their curiosity and interest. Taken together, these reasons for understanding make it worth the effort.

This is not to say that memorization is worthless. There will be times when Maurice's memorized knowledge solves the problem. In the same way, memorizing how to fasten a shoe lace is very useful. You do not need to understand knots to master shoe lace fastening and, since the fastening of shoe laces may be a daily occurrence, it serves a useful purpose. There is much in life that we might memorize without understanding. For instance, most people could get through life quite successfully and happily knowing how to fasten only a bow, a granny knot and a slip knot. For most of us, time could probably be better spent than in understanding knots. There are some people, however, like designers of weaving and knitting machines and mathematicians, who could find understanding knots to be both useful and interesting.

Given everything that might be understood in the world and the limited time each of us has in school, teaching must focus on understandings that we believe are important, enlightening, applicable, relevant and capable of enabling someone to live and work in a complex, technological society. This includes the understandings that help us grasp our place in the natural and physical world.

1.2 SOME KINDS OF UNDERSTANDING IN SCIENCE

The things we teach in science are usually associated with nature's patterns and regularities. For example, we might understand:

- *physical appearances or spatial arrangements*, as presented in a diagram of the solar system, the layers in the Earth, the organs of the human body, the divisions of an insect's body, the parts of a plant, and the shape of a shadow
- *properties*, such as hardness, opacity, roughness, conductivity
- *natural laws*, such as the way light reflects from a mirror
- *phenomena and events resulting from such properties and laws*, such as shadows, friction, echoes, why the ice cube has a bump on the top
- *conditions*, such as those needed for plants to grow and crystals to form
- *functions*, such as those of the lungs, heart and the bladder
- *processes*, such as melting, dissolving, decaying, growing and developing
- *procedures*, such the sequence of actions that will locate a fault in an electrical circuit or the steps in an investigation.

Figure 1.1 illustrates some aspects of science that could appear in an elementary science lesson. We can know these in different ways. For instance, we could know enough to name and describe the organs in the body and where they are situated. Similarly, we could describe the appearance of the crystal, and point out its regularities. We could describe how to help something dissolve by stirring it. We could describe the appearance and feel of the materials used to insulate a loft and we could tell someone what writing looks like in a mirror and that it can be read using a second mirror. But this is just a start. We could know, for instance, why I get a stitch when I run, why a crystal is so regular, why stirring can speed up dissolving, why loft insulation works and why a second mirror makes the image of writing in the first mirror look normal. In turn, these understandings may enable us to, for example, know how we might reduce the risk of certain lung diseases, explain how crystals 'grow', make a sweet last longer, choose a fabric to make a warm sweater and understand why AMBULANCE is printed oddly on the front of the vehicle.

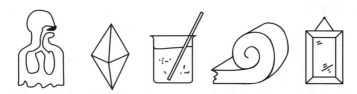

Figure 1.1 The arrangement of the body's organs, crystal formation, dissolving things, loft insulation, reflections in a mirror

Descriptive understanding

If children have a descriptive understanding of a topic, they can describe it. For instance, after a lesson about the solar system, they may be able to tell you what it is like on the surface of some of the planets. In some instances, it is as though they have constructed a mental 'picture' of what you want them to know. The actual words you used to describe the situation (the solar system) may be forgotten but the child is able to use the mental 'picture' and his or her own words to give you a meaningful account of it. In this way, children may know the physical arrangement of some of the organs in the human body and what they do, the relationship between the length of a shadow and the height of the sun, the supply of water to a plant and its survival, the angle of the ramp and the distance the truck travels, the predictable way that light reflects from a flat mirror, what is meant by hardness and melting and how to proceed in a particular investigation, as when finding the relative strength of different materials. With descriptive understanding, however, the reasons underpinning these may not be known. For instance, with only descriptive understanding, the child is unlikely to know why the stomach can digest food or why a thin wire carrying a large electrical current can become hot.

Explanatory understanding

If children have an explanatory understanding, they have a descriptive understanding of the situation *and* some relevant reasons or causes for it. They can, for instance, tell you that the moon has craters *because* it has been hit by lumps of rock from space. This means they can attempt to answer such questions as: Why is it like that? How did it arise? Why is it the way it is? For instance, with an explanatory understanding they can respond reasonably to such questions as: Why is a shadow always on the side furthest from the source of light? Why is a hedgehog prickly? What makes some things feel rough? What causes friction? What causes echoes? Why does a plant need light to survive? Why does a woollen scarf keep you warm? Why do things decay? Why does a steeper ramp make the toy truck go farther? Why does finding a break in a light bulb filament tell us it will not work in an electrical circuit? Understandings like these are sometimes neglected but they are one of the central aims of science. It is important that children learn that science is about more than naming and describing. They need to be introduced to reasons for things as they become capable of grasping them. This does not mean, of course, that reasons have to be complex. There are levels of explanation. For example, at one level, we might ask, 'How does a periscope work?' and provide an answer by drawing on our understanding of the way light reflects from a mirror. Children could probably grasp that. But children could also ask, 'Why does light reflect from a mirror like that?' They are unlikely to grasp the fundamental physical reasons for the regular reflection of light from a flat mirror. Instead, we might overcome that by drawing parallels with the way a ball bounces off a smooth wall, as in Figure 1.2.

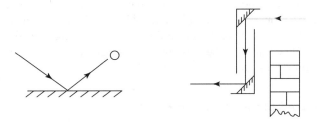

Figure 1.2 Light reflecting from a flat mirror like a ball bouncing off a wall and how a periscope lets us see over a wall

Procedural understanding

Procedural understanding is about grasping the way of doing something. In science, there are ways of using a hand lens and of carrying out an investigation. We expect children to learn both. The first might be a simple task while the second is developed over several years. Procedural understanding can be descriptive or explanatory. If, for instance, a child can tell you how to use a thermometer, his understanding is at least descriptive. If he can tell you why you should use it like that, the understanding is explanatory. The development of procedural understanding, often associated with scientific inquiry, exploring in a systematic way and testing ideas, is frequently a valued outcome of science teaching. Again, this kind of understanding can be descriptive or explanatory: you can know what to do only *or* you can know what to do *and* why it is appropriate to do it that way. Suppose a child wants to know what woodlice prefer to eat. She thinks they may eat damp soil, damp wood or damp straw because these were where she found them. She designs a test in which she places equal amounts of the possible foodstuffs at equal distances from her woodlice, which are under a box. At this point, this is evidence that she has at least some descriptive procedural understanding. She knows she should 'make things the same' (here, amounts and distances). This girl, however, can also give reasons for the equal amounts and distances. She can tell you that if they were not equal, it would not be fair. More than that, if one lot of food was closer than the others to the woodlice, they might go to that one because it was easier than going to the others. If one pile was bigger than the others, the woodlice might go to that one because they are greedy creatures or want to use it as a hiding place. This would be evidence of some explanatory procedural understanding. When she opens the box, she finds woodlice at all the materials. She is, however, cautious, and does not claim that the woodlice eat all these and gives a reason: 'They might just like to be where it's cool and damp'. This is further evidence of an explanatory procedural understanding of the investigation she is conducting. 'Mum's potted plants always die' illustrates how several kinds of understandings can be involved in a task.

Mum's potted plants always die

Mum just doesn't seem to have green fingers. Every time someone gives her a potted plant, it dies. She always waters it and stands the pots in sunlight. Why do the plants die? What is she doing wrong?

The children have to find out. First, it helps if they know something about the conditions plants generally need. This helps them to make reasonable suggestions for the cause of mum's failure with plants, rather than blind guesses. These children have that knowledge and have grown seedlings in pots. They are given some cress seeds and plant six in each of four yoghurt pots that contain damp potting compost. These seeds germinate and begin to grow.

In the meantime, the children look at one of mum's potted plants. The compost is wet and soggy. They suggest that mum's plants died because the plant's roots rotted because she had given them too much water. They have to test their idea.

The children place all the pots in sunlight and water them regularly. They give the first pot ten drops of water, the second gets twenty drops, the third gets thirty drops and the fourth gets forty drops each day. By the end of the week, the last one was dead. When the children took it from the pot, the compost was wet and soggy and the plant roots smelled awful and looked rotten. The children suggest that mum's plants die because she gives them too much water and so their roots rotted. It would be a good idea if mum gave her plants less water.

What kinds of understanding could be involved in this science task?

- First, the children need a descriptive understanding of the situation. What they see, read and hear has to make enough sense for them to grasp the situation well enough to describe it meaningfully. In this case, this is probably the easy part but it may not always be so. More than that, if some part does not make sense, they may ignore it and construct an understanding with the rest.
- Next, the children need to include a possible cause in that understanding. This makes the descriptive understanding into a possible explanation (explanatory understanding) of the situation. The cause they supplied was in the relationship between the amount of water and the plant's health: too much water made the plant die because the roots rotted in the water.
- Finally, the children may also understand the procedure that was used in the investigation. For instance, you would probably want them to understand the reason for using matching pots and for standing them in the same conditions.

Facts, figures and understandings

In our everyday lives, we acquire a lot of knowledge, even without trying. Some of it amounts to facts, figures and similar snippets of information. Some amounts to descriptive understandings, some to explanatory understandings and some to procedural understandings of both kinds. If you cast your mind over a recent day's experience, you can probably find examples of all of these. Jotting them down may help you focus your thoughts.

- facts (for example, new relationships, the shop with the sale on)

- figures (telephone numbers, meeting times and dates, test results)

- descriptive understanding (for example, the layout of some-one's new flat)

- explanatory understanding (involving reasons or causes; for example, why John did so badly in yesterday's test)

- descriptive procedural understanding (for example, how to reach the shop with the sale on)

- explanatory procedural understanding (involving reasons or causes; for example, how to jump start your car and why the procedure is appropriate)

Facts, figures and understandings in science

Here are some aspects of science that you may have to teach. As you read them, think of the understandings that you could expect children to develop. Would there be:

- descriptive understanding?
- explanatory understanding, involving reasons or causes?
- procedural understanding, not involving reasons or causes?
- procedural understanding, involving reasons or causes?
- or none of these?

- The names of the planets.
- An eclipse.
- Where the wisdom teeth are.
- Elasticity.
- The life cycle of a butterfly.
- Separating a mixture of a soluble and an insoluble substance (such as sand and salt).
- Testing the idea that running water can cause soil to be eroded.
- Sorting objects into metals and other materials.

Focusing on understandings

Teaching often supports particular kinds of learning in a lesson. Here are five lessons on different topics. What kind or kinds of understanding (if any) do these lessons seem most likely to support?

- descriptive understanding
- explanatory understanding, involving reasons or causes
- procedural understanding, not involving reasons or causes
- procedural understanding, involving reasons or causes
- none of these

The naming of parts

The children are shown an entire plant. They examine its roots, stem, leaves and its flower. They are given a worksheet that has a picture of the plant with arrows pointing to various parts. They colour the picture and label the parts.

Testing threads

Children are sometimes set the task of testing a variety of threads to find the strongest. They follow the rule that the conditions should be the same for all threads and, after testing them, can tell the teacher which was the strongest thread.

Change

The topic is *Change* but the children do not distinguish between *melting* and *dissolving*. When watching the teacher melt chocolate on the radiator, they correctly called it melting. When stirring a sugar cube in water, they also described what happened to the sugar as melting. The teacher had them look closely and see the sugar disappear into the water. With the chocolate, the heat made it runny but it did not mix with anything. The children said that bits of sugar 'soaked' off into the water but the bits of chocolate 'just ran down'.

Forces

The topic is *Forces* and the teacher showed the children a toy car on a level table and asked how they might make it move. After they went through the obvious ways, such as 'Push it' and 'Hit it', they began to explore less commonplace possibilities. One was to attach a pencil sharpener to a thread, hang it over the edge of the table and attach the other end of the thread to the car. When they released the pencil sharpener, the car quickly built up speed as it crossed the table. The teacher seized the opportunity and asked them what difference it would make if they fastened another car to the first one. 'It would go faster', they predicted. 'Why do you think that?' she asked. 'Because there are more wheels now', was their reason. They were really puzzled when they tested their idea and found the car built up speed very slowly. They thought something was wrong with the wheels but the same thing happened with other cars. When they attached a third car, the three cars built up speed even more slowly. Eventually, they decided that the more cars there are, the more slowly they build up speed. It was probably the first inverse relationship they had ever consciously explored.

Energy

The teacher asked the children what makes them move. 'Muscles', they recalled. 'But, what makes muscles move?' he persisted. 'Energy, from oxygen in the air and food; they make energy in our muscles', they recalled. 'How does oxygen and things from food get into our muscles?' he asked. They remembered that they are carried there in the blood. 'But what makes the blood move?' he persisted. 'The heart', they replied, confidently. 'When do you think you will need a lot of energy for your muscles?' 'When we are running about', they answered. 'So, if you were to run up the stairs to the first landing, what do you think would happen to your heart rate?' They predicted correctly. 'Why?' he followed through. They explained that the muscles would need more energy, so they would need a greater flow of blood and that would mean the heart would have to beat faster. 'What will happen if you run all the way up to the second landing?' They again made a reasoned prediction. 'Let's test it and see if that really happens', he concluded. The children designed fair tests and did their experiments.

1.3 GETTING TO KNOW THE UNDERSTANDINGS YOU WILL SUPPORT

If you have a clear idea of the kinds of understanding you want from a lesson, it helps you direct your efforts towards them. It gives you a clear target and also tells you what to look for at the end of the lesson. But we generally do not carry *all* the knowledge that we need to teach in our heads. Even someone with a background in science does not know everything that could be known about all the branches of science, or even everything about one branch. You may already have had to check on one or two bits of science yourself when you were thinking about some of the things that appeared earlier. Having knowledge and understanding to begin with may save some time but it still has to be translated into a form that suits your class. So, if you are a little unsure of the topic yourself, what do you do?

Most teachers develop their knowledge on an as need basis, usually as they plan their lessons. For a variety of reasons, they may do no more than look for practical activities and put together some sort of worksheet to practise what is learned. For instance, in a topic on electricity, this activity could be to follow instructions to set up a circuit to light a bulb and then note the effect of variations in that circuit. The worksheet has the children draw the circuit, name the parts and state what happens as the circuit is altered. At best, this is only as start. To do more, you may need some good source materials, such as one or two books at the children's level. You may also need one at a slightly higher level that you can use as a handbook. At least one of these books should contain everyday examples of scientific concepts and events. One should contain ideas to talk about and activities you might adapt for the children. When you select your source materials, guard against those that give only facts, figures and descriptions. You also want reasons and causes. Why, for instance, does there have to be a complete circuit for the bulb to light? Your colleagues are also resources but, unlike your handbook, they will expect consideration. Here is a routine that you might use. With understanding in mind:

- Find the topic in your books, looking for clear descriptions and explanations.
- State what the understandings are that you will support in direct and unambiguous terms (take care not to neglect explanatory understanding when it is within the grasp of the children; if necessary, look for simple ways of supporting this understanding).

- List some everyday examples that you will introduce, show or talk about with the children.
- Choose one or more activities to support that understanding; you may have to modify one so that it does the task you want.
- If you prepare a worksheet or set some questions to answer, make sure they are to do with the understandings you want to support (descriptive and explanatory). If you do not, the children may come to believe that only facts and descriptions count in science.
- Keep your ideas to save you time in the future.

Planning for understanding

Here are two examples of lessons being developed that aim to support explanatory understandings as well as descriptive understandings; the first is for younger children and the second for older children.

The rough and the smooth

Suppose you have to teach the children the concepts of rough and smooth. What understandings could be involved?

Obvious questions are: Why are these things rough and those things smooth? What makes some things rough and other things smooth? Why does being rough or smooth matter? The children's book has a section on friction. It shows a magnified view of a rough, uneven surface with lots of spiky bits that could catch as you try to slide your hand over it. There is also a close-up picture of a smooth surface for comparison. You decide that a simple understanding of the cause of friction is within the grasp of the children. More specifically, you want the children to be able to explain what makes a surface feel rough or feel smooth and predict (not guess) whether a surface will offer a lot of friction or a little friction. You also want them to be able to relate this to some everyday instances of the effects of friction.

You collect some rough and smooth materials and some hand magnifiers. A colleague has a large picture of a room showing a variety of materials in use and you borrow it. First, you plan to have the children acquire the concept 'smooth' from direct contact with some smooth objects (literally, hands-on). Next, they will discriminate between things which feel smooth and things which do not feel smooth, hence introducing the idea of roughness. At this point, you will introduce the hand magnifiers and the children will compare the surfaces and describe them, relating what they see to what they feel. They will try to push objects across the surfaces and explain why some move more easily than others. Places where we want smoothness (for example, a playground slide) and places where we want roughness (for example, on slippery steps) are examined. The lesson will conclude with a discussion about the smooth and the rough things shown in the large picture and why they are suited to their purpose.

Crystals

Suppose you want the children to know something about Earth Science. Some of the rocks you have to show them contain obvious, well-shaped crystals. In the past, you have talked about the appearance of crystals and gem stones. What understandings could be involved?

One obvious why question is: Why do crystals have regular shapes with straight edges and flat sides? You want the children to understand why this is and be able to explain it. You look in your children's book and find it shows pictures of crystals but does not explain their regular shape. In your 'handbook' you find that the regularity is due to the way the tiny particles of the material fit together. There is a diagram showing how polystyrene balls pile up to make a pyramid when poured into a small tray. You decide that this is within the grasp of the children you teach.

You take the book with pictures in it, remind yourself to wear the ring with that enormous cubic zirconia in it, sort out the rocks that show the crystals most clearly, and find a bag of marbles and a small cardboard lid from a box to serve as a tray. When you mention it to another teacher, he says he has the materials and instructions for growing a big crystal of alum. You make a mental note about how and where you will set this up so the children can see it but not touch or taste it. All that remains is to write a worksheet. You plan to ask the children to explain how they think a crystal can 'grow'. You will remind them of the marbles-in-the-lid analogy and have a larger lid ready to stand the first one in. This is to help them see that extra layers of marbles may be added to the sides of the pyramid to make it bigger while keeping its basic shape.

Getting to know the understandings in a topic

The best way to appreciate what is involved is to try it for yourself. Choose from the following topics and practise getting to know the understandings that you will support. Time is always short so we need efficient ways of preparing a lesson that includes reasons and causes when appropriate.

Topics to choose from

Care for the environment	Shadows
Comparing people with other animals	Skeletons
Germs and healthy living	Solids, liquids and gases
Loudness of sound	The scientist
Musical instruments	The seasons
Pollution	Transparency

For the topic of your choice, research and prepare a lesson outline, something like the one described in 'The rough and the smooth' or in 'Crystals'.

1.4 SCIENTIFIC LANGUAGE

Before going further, there needs to be a word about words. It is easy to be obscure in science, all you have to do is choose your words and string them together – science will even show you how. What we need to be, of course, is considerate.

To some degree, the language of science has become ritualized, that is, a way of talking and writing has evolved that has become the accepted norm for communicating in science. You do not find scientists beginning a report of their work for other scientists with, 'As I got out of bed this morning, I had this idea and I went straight to my lab and . . .' It would be returned immediately for revision. However, behind the ritualized language is an orientation towards the world, a disposition or scientific attitude that we want children to develop in their science lessons. This involves seeking rational explanations, justifying assertions reasonably, being open to and fair to ideas and appealing to, relying on and giving due weight to observation and experiment.

But it is not our aim to impress children with whatever facility we have with the language of science or to insist that they parrot it back to us. Instead, we need to draw them into it slowly, carefully develop their capacity to use it and, above all else, make sure that what we say and what they say is meaningful to them. The science the children do must be accessible to them. They are likely to find that abstraction, jargon, specialist vocabulary and the passive tense are obstructions. Eventually, they will overcome them but, in the meantime, you will have to take it into account. This generally means you should use a form of language that is grasped relatively quickly and you should introduce and support new structures and words carefully. Scientific language comprises more than words with special meanings. It tends to be concise and can be very abstract. For instance, children are likely to be familiar with 'the moving car'. Science, though, concerns itself with 'motion'. This steps away from the here and now, away from the toy car that is moving across the table, to movement in general. It also uses some language structures that children tend not to use in their everyday talk. These, for instance, describe relationships such as the way a massive object builds up speed more slowly than a less massive one, assuming the forces on them both are the same. Even translated into child–speak, the relationship and condition still have to be grasped: the lorry builds up speed more slowly than before because we have piled things up on it, even if the engine works just as hard. A child has to grasp the words that point to a relationship or condition, like 'when', 'if', 'because', 'so' and 'even if'.

As well as relational structures that are rather testing, there are ways of looking at the world that can seem strange to a child. Just because a child can recall a word and use it as you did does not necessarily mean that the child knows what it means.

One way of addressing people that is known to be effective is to direct what you say to them personally and relate it to their experiences. Compare, for example, 'Water runs downhill' with, 'The water you saw in the river was running downhill'. Similarly, compare, 'What effect does a lot of friction have on the force needed to move a heavy object?' with, 'How hard would you have to push that heavy box on this rough carpet, where there will be a lot of friction?' This form of expression can make the way you speak simpler and it has a very useful bonus – it can increase the children's attention.

Being considerate also means supporting the comprehension of technical and scientific words. Science has its own vocabulary of words with very precise meanings. These words are not all of the same kind. Some are already a part of the children's everyday language and have everyday meanings that can help understanding in science. Take *force*, for example. We might suggest that someone tries to force a cork into a bottle. We mean, of course, that they should apply a powerful push or twist to the cork. In elementary science, we often describe a force as a push, pull or twist. At this early stage, the everyday meaning provides a bridge to the scientific meaning. This approximation makes the science accessible to young children. Having made the term meaningful, the way is open to refine it. Note that there are also other meanings of *force* that may be less helpful as, for instance, in the forcing of plants where no direct pull, push or twist is involved. Although care must be taken not to propagate inappropriate meanings, translating scientific language into simple, familiar terms that maintain the integrity of the science can be very helpful to children. In this way, new ideas can be related to what is already well known and, in the process, gain meaning.

Other everyday words may seem to share meanings with science but the differences may be less obvious and can be very important. Although words like *energy, pressure, power* and *heat* are in common use, their meanings are not quite the same in science. For instance, in the vernacular, a lack of energy can describe a feeling of lassitude. A change of mood might be sufficient to make you energetic. In scientific terms, the level of energy that was available to you was much the same in both states and probably derives from what you ate at breakfast. Similarly, in everyday language, we might say that what we ate was full of energy, as though the gaps in the tiny bits of cereal were filled with a special substance called energy. Scientifically, of course, what we eat is neither full nor empty of energy. Instead, it is how its bits and pieces are arranged that counts. It would be easy for a child to transfer everyday meanings to the scientific world. For instance, a child could describe a piece of coal as full of energy – and mean it quite literally. In this sense, everyday meanings can mislead and a child needs to learn that the same word can mean different things in different domains. Similarly, concrete examples can add enormously to meaning and can serve as reference points for the future. For example, when an elastic band is stretched, its bits are pulled apart. When we release the band, it returns to its original shape. We could use the band to make a toy buggy move as the band returns to its original shape. What counts is how the bits and pieces of the elastic band are arranged. The more we stretch it, the more energy there is available. The point is that the rubber band is a concrete object that children can see and feel and observe in action.

Science also includes words with meanings that were once well known but, in everyday use, no longer mean the same. For instance, *charge* as in *charge a balloon with static electricity by rubbing it* is used in the sense of charging (filling) a glass with wine. When scientists like Benjamin Franklin studied static electricity, some thought of electricity as something you could pour into a bottle. In this sense, to charge a balloon means to top it up with electricity. For a child today, it could mean that the balloon is expected to make a payment. Such words, reflecting an earlier way of thinking about a topic, have become living fossils.

Science also uses words coined for the occasion. For example, *spectrum* and *food chain* describe particular phenomena and concepts in science. Children often acquire new words readily and use them as intended but their experience is frequently limited. Becoming familiar with scientific terms can take more time and use than some allow. Children need opportunities to use the terms in a variety of situations so that meanings can be refined, narrowed or widened and become a genuine part of their specialized vocabulary. A cursory introduction to the 'correct' word and then allowing children to choose it from a menu when supplying missing words in sentences is unlikely to be enough. At the same time, it is important that an exploration of meaning is not suffocated by pedantry and unreasonable expectations.

Potentially more of a problem are words that are familiar to children but have subtly different meanings in science. For example, *gas* is a scientific word that has entered into everyday language. It is related to *chaos*, the Greek word for disorder, and was chosen by the Belgian chemist, Van Helmont, to describe the chaotic way that particles are arranged in, for instance, air. The word is now in common use but children may tie it to a particular gas, such as that used for heating in the home. When talking about a gas in science, we refer, of course, to a state that all materials have if they are hot enough. When you use the word, do the children think you are referring to a particular gas that is commonly used as a fuel? Another example is in the way we commonly distinguish between *people, farm animals, pets, wild animals* and *insects* but, in science, they are all *animals*. Similarly, science describes as *plants* what people call *trees, soft herbaceous plants, grass* and '*green stuff on the fence*' (the single-celled protococcus). When you refer to animals or plants, what frameworks are children using to interpret what you say? Do they exclude people and insects from the former and trees from the latter? Distinctions of this kind are easily overlooked because of a superficial resemblance between the children's concepts and those of science.

There are various things a teacher might do to help children construct meaning and learn when a particular meaning is appropriate. These include:

- When introducing scientific terms, using more familiar terms first then pairing them with the scientific terms afterwards, slowly withdrawing the support provided by the familiar terms. (For example, we might begin by using the words *squashed* or *crushed* and quickly pair it with *compressed*. Later, we use *compressed* but mention *squashed* or *crushed* to remind the children of the link. After a while, we would use only *compressed* but expect the children to tell us the link words.)
- Identifying everyday examples of the scientific term and then introducing discrimination. (For example, *This is a pulling force, look. Find me another one . . . and another one. . . . This is a pushing force . . . Find me another one . . . and another one . . .; Look at these; there are pulling forces and pushing forces; which is which?*)
- Expecting the children to translate scientific language into familiar talk and vice versa. (For example, *Yes, I think I would agree with you. You said it was a food web. Tell us what a food web is? Why do scientists call it a web? Yes, I understand. Can anyone explain it in another way? The more ways we have, the better.*)
- Having the children use new scientific terms (and continue to use those acquired earlier) in different contexts and in different ways. (For example, after children test the effect of different surfaces on the motion of a toy car, they are expected to discuss the motion of a feather falling in air using similar terms. Another example is: *Invent a sentence with the word force in it, used like a scientist would use it. Good.*

Now invent another sentence with the word force in it. The more different it is the more I'll like it. Sometimes it may be possible to give the children several sentences using the target term and have them identify correct and incorrect uses of it.)

- Teaching the children when the scientific term is appropriate in their talk and writing. (For example, *Now, I want you to write about your experiment like a scientist would. What do you think that means? Tell me the important words you will have to use.*)

You may not replace or eradicate the everyday meanings of terms that a child has acquired. In reality, old and new meanings may exist side by side, one to be used in an everyday context and the other in science. The aim is to strengthen the latter and connect it to what is understood well to produce a more coherent whole. With use, the scientific understandings should grow in strength and area of application. The following example illustrates the development of meaning for a term that is used in science.

Helping children grasp the meaning of 'pattern' in science

Science seeks patterns in nature and tries to explain them (Figure 1.3), but what do we mean by a *pattern* in nature? One way of helping children construct a meaning for the expression could be to:

1 Have children examine manufactured patterns (such as on wallpapers and fabrics, in the ways regular objects are packaged, in a brick wall, on a tiled roof, in mechanical structures; see also Figure 1.3).

   Some familiar talk: *Which bits happen over and over again? If it happens over and over the same way, it's a pattern. Is this a pattern? Why is it not a pattern? Do you know any other patterns? Tell us about one.*

Figure 1.3 Patterns on a wallpaper, in a snail shell, in the arrangement of petals, in a snowflake, on a ladybird

2   Have children make patterns themselves (by making potato prints, making regular structures with art straws).
Some familiar talk: *Which bits happen over and over again? (Which parts repeat over and over again?) What makes it a pattern? Tell everyone how you made your pattern so perfect.*

3   Have children look for naturally occurring patterns (the growth rings in a cross-section of a tree, a spider's web, a snail shell, petals on a buttercup; see also Figure 1.3).
Some familiar talk: *Are these patterns as 'good' as the ones you made? How are they different? Is it a perfect pattern? What would it have to be like to be perfect? I wonder if the world is full of patterns? Do you know any more? Tell us about one? What parts repeat? Is it a perfect pattern? What would it look like if it was perfect?*

4   Describe a behavioural pattern to the children (for example, we get up, have breakfast, go to school, have lessons, etc., and this repeats, day after day).
Some familiar talk: *There are other kinds of patterns we can look for. They are not like the ones we found on wallpaper or the ones we made in potato prints. These are things that are the same every time they happen. Here's an example: (a description of a behavioural pattern familiar to the children). Are there any other patterns like this you can think of? Tell us about one. What is it that makes it a pattern? What is it that happens over and over again (repeats)?*

5   Have children examine other regularities in the way nature behaves (as in the way light reflects from a mirror, the way the diameter of the patch of light from a torch changes as the distance from the wall increases, the way the length of an elastic band and the note it makes are related).
Some familiar talk: *What is the same every time you do it? What is the pattern you have found (what is it that repeats)? This is what scientists do, they look for patterns like these and try to explain what makes them.*

Being familiar

Read the following sets of statements and, as you do so, try expressing them in simple, familiar terms. You should aim to be as near the original meaning as you can. In each case, also consider what meaning has been lost or changed, if any, when expressed in more familiar terms.

- Sound is caused by vibration.
  Sound reverberates in a large, empty room.
  Sound is absorbed by fabrics in a room.

- Friction opposes motion.
  Some liquids are viscous.
  Lubrication reduces friction.

- The earth rotates on its axis.
  The moon revolves around the earth.
  The vacuum of space.

- Plant.
  Microbe.
  Habitat.

Making meaning

To appreciate what is involved in making language meaningful, try it for yourself. Choose one of the following scientific expressions and devise a way of making it more meaningful for children. Think of familiar words you could use to support the process.

- a fair test
- care for the environment
- characteristics of living things
- a gas

1.5 CUMULATIVE SUMMARY

This part has described the importance of having an understanding and has pointed to some kinds of understanding that are central to science. Knowing what your targets are helps you focus on them in your lessons. One or two books that give attention to the key relationships that are appropriate for the age you teach will help. You will also need to identify language that is likely to hinder learning and think of ways of making it meaningful.

The next part is about some kinds of talk that will support children's learning in science. This talk aims to establish understandings that can be developed further. It includes a look at the potential of talk in practical activity as this is an important place where a variety of understandings and scientific attitudes may be developed. Figure 1.4 is the beginning of a chart that collects the suggestions so far into the first step. This chart will be updated after each part.

```
┌─────────────────────────────┐
│  Step 1                     │
│                             │
│  Get to know the topic.     │
│                             │
│  Be clear about the         │
│  understandings you want.   │
│                             │
│  Think about how to treat   │
│  the scientific language.   │
└─────────────────────────────┘
```

Figure 1.4 Summary chart

Part 2

Helping children understand: guiding thought

This part describes some early steps in supporting children's thinking processes to increase the likelihood that they will begin to understand the science. To some extent, these amount to helping children make relevant mental connections. To this end, they are prepared for the topic and then helped to notice relationships in it. During this time, you will need to monitor the quality of their learning so that is also discussed. Practical activity is often an inseparable part of science teaching so how to make the most of it using talk is considered, too. While children may have the ability to make the necessary mental connections, they may not use it. Pressing for understanding obliges children to use their ability so that they are more likely to establish an understanding. The nature of a press for understanding and how to apply it is described. In places, oral interaction between a teacher and the children is used to illustrate certain points. In these, *T* indicates the teacher's talk and *C* indicates the children's talk.

2.1 GUIDING THOUGHT

Although you cannot make someone understand, you can point them in the right direction, make sure they have relevant knowledge, help them develop it into a suitable form, and make connections, patterns and relationships hard to miss. In effect, you are guiding the direction their thoughts take. This means that there must be some thinking going on for you to shape and guide. The age old way of doing this is to ask questions, as Socrates is said to have done over 2000 years ago when he wanted to make his students think. Of course, they have to be the right questions. If you ask for facts, the mind will tend to concern itself with facts but, if you ask for relationships, reasons and causes, then thinking is more likely to be aimed at constructing relationships, reasons and causes.

Sometimes, you may need to ask for facts, at other times you will focus attention on relationships, reasons and causes. Sometimes, the talk will relate to prior experience and, at other times, it will be about something the children have just seen or are investigating. This does not mean, however, that you must launch a barrage of 'hard' questions at the children or act like some Inquisition interrogator. Nor does it mean that every time you speak, it has to be to ask a question. Your guiding discourse may, and probably will, include questions but it does not have to be entirely questions. Talk should focus on what is needed to move learning forward. If that means it needs a question, then ask that question; if it means it needs a statement, then make the statement. Whatever the form of the talk, the overriding aim is to push the children's thinking forward and press for understanding.

Your talk with the children will also reveal existing understandings that you may build on. For example, a child is likely to arrive with an understanding that animals and people have some things in common: they move, breathe, eat and excrete and they both can see, hear, feel and smell. You may draw attention to other similarities, perhaps by showing pictures of skeletons and internal organs. On other occasions, however, existing understandings may hinder what you want to teach. For example, children may believe that electricity comes from a battery and is consumed by a light bulb. This may make it more difficult for them to grasp the reasons for a complete circuit. You need to know when the children have such an understanding so that you can address it.

Pushing thinking forward

Fostering understanding can be thought of as supporting children's thinking so that they construct a meaningful mental 'picture' of some situation or event. In science, it cannot be just any mental 'picture'; it has to be one that is at least on the way to being acceptable to the scientific community. Just as an artist may need a pencil to begin with and a brush to complete the picture, so the learner may need one kind of support to start the process and a different kind to complete it. Focused talk is oral interaction that is tailored to suit the particular needs of a learner at a particular stage in his or her construction of an understanding. Focused talk is not, however, meant to be a monologue for transmitting information to the children. Three major kinds of focused talk will be described in what follows: tuning-talk, connecting-talk and monitoring-talk. Each has an important task.

Tuning-talk

At the beginning of a lesson on the loudness of sound you might say that you were nearly deafened by the noise of the low-flying aircraft that just flew over the school. You ask them to listen to the noise of a pin dropping on the floor and compare it with the aircraft's noise. You might follow that by asking the children for other examples of loud and quiet noises that they know. Finally, you ask what they think today's science lesson will be about. You confirm it will be about loud and quiet noises and add that, today, they will be finding out the best way of protecting our hearing from really loud noises.

Before you start the lesson, the children's thoughts may be on anything but the topic in hand. You need to tune them in, make their mental resources available to them, check the quality of those resources and, perhaps, do a few repairs then point them towards what matters first. Your interaction with the children will be directed towards these ends. The interaction about sound described above is an example of such tuning-talk. In general, tuning-talk will probably relate to the following.

- *Setting the scene.* This aim is to draw children's attention to the context or broad area in which the specific topic is embedded. It is to help the child recall relevant previous knowledge and experience. Whatever is learned in the lesson is, ultimately, to be tied to this broader network of knowledge, making it more meaningful and durable.

- *Making prior knowledge and understanding accessible.* This aims to draw specific knowledge and experiences that are relevant into each child's active thoughts. Children should be encouraged to reveal existing understandings.
- *Checking its quality and making it sufficient for the current purpose.* This aims to check that the relevant prior knowledge is adequate for its purpose and, if it is not, to develop or change it to make it so. When existing understandings are likely to impede further learning, they will need further attention.
- *Stating the aim of the lesson.* This tells the children where they will be going and sensitizes them to information and cues that fulfil the aim. It may be necessary to remind children of the aim later in the lesson.
- *Focusing attention on those specific aspects of the topic where you will begin.* This aims to bring the children's attention to the first step of the lesson.

The precise form of the tuning-talk depends on what is to be taught and on the age, abilities, prior knowledge and experience of the children concerned. On some occasions, the tuning-talk may be relatively brief. For instance, suppose you intend to ask older children to make a torch as a problem-solving test of learning. Available are some wires, a battery, a light bulb in a holder and a cardboard tube. You might set the scene, outline the aim, focus attention on some specific points and let them try it. If they show their existing understanding to be inadequate, you would probably intervene with some focused talk that helps them organize and extend their knowledge. On the other hand, beginning a new topic like *Animal camouflage* with young children may need an extensive introduction which uses most or all of the kinds of tuning-talk listed above. You could, for instance, have them talk about their game of hide and seek and how not to be seen by blending in with the background. You may describe hides used to observe wildlife and have the children recall other instances of camouflage that they know. After this tuning-talk, you may introduce a practical task in which the children search for coloured counters you threw over a patch of grass earlier and relate the outcome to animals that live among foliage, like the greenfly aphid.

Some tuning-talk

Here are some teachers guiding thinking in science. Notice particularly the emphasis on tuning-talk at this stage of the lesson. You will be able to spot it as you read what is said. 'Heat insulation' is a lesson with younger children; 'Floating and sinking' is a lesson with older children. (You may find it useful to underline the tuning-talk.)

A lesson on the properties of materials – heat insulation

T: 'Think about this morning. Think about when you came to school. [Pause.] What was it like? Was it warm or cold?'

C: 'It was cold. I could see my breath.'

T: 'Yes, it was cold, wasn't it? [Pause, while everyone agrees.] What do you wear when it's cold?'

C: 'A coat.'

T: 'Yes, a coat. [Pause.] Do you wear anything else to keep you warm?'

C: 'A scarf and some gloves. Mine are on the radiator.'

T: 'That's right. A scarf and gloves will keep you warm. How many of you came with scarves this morning? [Pause.] Yes, a lot of you came with scarves so that you would be warm. [Pause.]I've brought some of my scarves. How many have I got? [Takes answer.] Which scarf do you think will keep me really warm. Which do you think will be the best one for a really cold day?'

C: 'The red one. It's red.'

T: 'So you think the red one will be best. Why do you think that?'

C: 'Because it's red. I've got a red one. Mine . . . my scarf is warm.'

T: 'Thank you, Fiona. Well, you might be right. Let's all see your scarf. Look, everyone. Fiona's scarf does look a warm one. Why do you think it's warm. [Pause.] Alison?'

C: 'Because it's fluffy.'

T: 'It is fluffy. Is my red scarf fluffy, too? John?' [Pause.]

C: 'Yes.'

T: 'It is, isn't it? Well, what we are going to do is find out if it really is the best scarf for keeping warm. What are we going to do, Peter?' [Takes response.]

Much of this interaction could be called tuning-talk. For example, there is the exchange beginning with: 'Think about this morning' (intended to orientate the children towards the topic in hand) and 'Which scarf do you think will be the best one?' (intended to bring out prior knowledge about the insulating properties of materials).

A lesson on the properties of materials – floating and sinking

The teacher puts the title, *Floating and Sinking*, on the board and asks the children what they think today's science lesson is going to be about.

C: 'Things that float and sink.'

T: 'Yes. Tell me something that floats.'

C: 'A ship.'

T: 'And something that sinks?'

C: 'A stone.'

T: 'Good. Can anyone think of something that can float *and* sink?'

C: 'A submarine.'

T: 'Very good. Watch, I'm going to put some things in this dish of water. [A toy car is placed in the water and it sinks to the bottom of the dish.] Did it float or sink?'

C: 'Sink.' [The teacher now places a plastic duck in the water and looks up enquiringly.]

C: 'Float.'

T: 'Good. What about this?' [He places a block of wood in the water which settles so that barely a millimetre is above the water.]

C: 'Sinks . . . No! It's floating. Well, maybe . . . No, that's sunk.' [The teacher knows that he will need to clarify what is meant by floating and sinking before he can proceed with the lesson. This he does by example and then he continues.]

T: 'Now then, what about this?' [The teacher holds up an empty, sealed jar.]

C: 'It'll float', suggest the children. [The teacher demonstrates that the response is correct.]

T: 'Why?'

C: 'Because it's got air in it. Everything with air in floats.'

T: 'So will this float?' [He holds up another empty, sealed jar and, when they say it will, he places it in the water and it sinks.] 'Now there's a problem! How do you explain that?' [The children move closer and stare at the sunken jar in disbelief.]

Simply asking the children what they think today's science lesson is going to be about begins the process of tuning their minds to the task in hand. Asking for examples strengthens that and gives the teacher some insight into the quality and quantity of their prior knowledge. Two understandings that could impede progress were revealed. The first was the children's understanding of what is meant by the word 'floating' and the second was a belief that all air-filled, hollow objects will float. The teacher expected the latter and used it to surprise and attract interest.

Planning your own tuning-talk

To appreciate what is involved, try planning some tuning-talk to prepare your class for a lesson on some properties of natural materials.

If your interest is in teaching younger children, the topic is:

*   Not all stones are the same

If your interest is in teaching older children, the topic is:

*   Soils

Connecting-talk

Connecting-talk is focused talk that helps children make mental connections. It guides their thinking and directs attention to what matters to increase the likelihood that they will make those mental connections. In science, we want the children to notice patterns, relationships, reasons and causes. The connecting-talk should help them do that. Here are some examples.

In a lesson on shadows, the children watch how a stick's shadow changes as time passes. You direct their attention to its position and the position of the sun. You repeat this at intervals and ask why the shadow has moved. They tell you it is because the clouds are moving. You have them look at their own shadow and note the position of the sun relative to the shadow. You do it again later. You ask which way the shadow moved. You also ask which way the sun moved. What will happen to the sun if we wait? Which way will it move? Can they tell you where the shadow will be then? You return to one of the lesson's targets, 'So, why does the shadow move?' As these are younger children, you structure the response for them, 'The shadow moves this way *because . . .*'

On another occasion, after you have completed your tuning-talk and are into your lesson on seed dispersal, you pass out some double-winged seeds to the class and focus their attention on the wings. 'What do you think these bits are for?' You do not receive a clear response so you refocus by asking what they look like. The children say they look like aeroplane wings. You ask what wings are for and the children tell you they are for flying. With a little further talk, the children decide that the seed may be able to glide like a paper aeroplane. They try it and are gratified to find it does. You have them test seeds to see how far they glide when released from different heights. As they do it, you ask what they are doing, what the aim is, and why they are doing it like that. You now move in on a key understanding and ask why having winged seeds could be a good thing for a tree.

In the shadows lesson, an important causal connection was to be made between the changing position of the sun and the changing position of the shadow. The children were to understand that the latter was the cause of the former. The teacher's connecting-talk repeatedly directed attention to the parts of the situation that mattered. More than that, it was done in a systematic way. Attention was directed to the things to be connected (shadow position – sun position) one after the other, with nothing else intervening. The teacher cannot make the mental connection for the children but he or she can increase the chance that they will notice the relationship for themselves. This is reinforced by asking the children to predict where the shadow will be after some time has passed. To respond, the children have to construct a theory that involves cause and effect. In the seed dispersal lesson, attention was focused on the parts that mattered – the wings. The children were helped to draw on prior knowledge of wings to make a tentative connection between the appearance of the seed and its likely behaviour. The likelihood that the children would make the connection between having wing-like appendages and gliding away from the parent tree was increased by talk about the purpose of the wings and by the practical work. Making the more general connection between the ability to disperse and the advantages it gives the tree was supported by drawing on the specific case of this winged seed.

Connecting-talk may appear in any part of a lesson, even in an introduction if you found the children's existing knowledge needs to be developed. Your lesson will, however, have a message – something new that has to be grasped today. This is often expressed as the aim of, reason for or learning target of the lesson.

When children have inappropriate frameworks to guide their thinking, they may attend to things that are not relevant and even propagate misconceptions among other children. For instance, some of the children watching the stick's shadow thought it was the moving clouds that made the shadow move. They have their thoughts fixed on moving clouds, not the sun. This could reduce the likelihood that they will connect the sun's behaviour with that of the shadow. More than that, they can convince others that the moving clouds idea is a good one! The directing-of-attention role of connecting-talk is, therefore, very important. Some areas where connecting-talk can be useful are the following.

- *Constructing a coherent explanation.* Children might be expected to explain an observation, event or situation. This often means making a connection between what they perceive to be the effect with what they think is its cause. Is the effect they see the same as the one you see? Is their cause a plausible, well-founded one? Connecting-talk directs attention and helps the child develop what counts as an explanation. Talk and action are aimed at making reasons, causes, patterns, connections and relationships apparent, more obvious, more likely to be noticed. For instance, a child who sees coloured patterns on animals only as something that makes them look attractive may fail to connect the difficulty in seeing a tiger in long grass with its stripes. Similarly, children may not connect the drab appearance of a moth on a dirty tree trunk with an increased likelihood of its survival. You may have to show that colours can camouflage an object by, for instance, throwing a known number of small pieces of green string on an area of grass. The children find as many as they can in a minute. Why have they missed so many? They are then invited to consider the advantage of being a green caterpillar on grass and relate this to the survival of drab moths on dirty bark.

- *Generating ideas for practical activity.* This overlaps with the first area but has been separated to emphasize certain points. There are times when we want children to suggest tentative explanations, reasons or possible causes of events. These are what they could test or investigate in practical work (assuming that they lend themselves to practical investigation at this level). Connecting-talk can help them develop their ideas so that the children clearly grasp the reasons or causal connections they contain. It can also help the children make clear, rational predictions based on their ideas. During practical work, it can be used to remind them of their objectives. Later, it helps them identify patterns in their observations, data or findings and connect those patterns with their ideas and the reason for the investigation.

- *Applying/using new understandings in a variety of situations.* Connecting-talk here aims to support the consolidation, development and widening of a new and, perhaps, as yet, delicate understanding. Children may practise using their understandings by explaining very similar events then explaining events in different contexts or by making predictions about what will happen in different circumstances. Connecting-talk can be used to focus attention on what matters in the different contexts and highlight the connections that are to be made. You will probably become progressively less helpful as the children's understanding develops. Connecting-talk may also support the making of links between a new understanding and other areas of knowledge. The aim is to embed the new understanding firmly in the web of existing knowledge.

Some connecting-talk

Looking back at 'Some tuning-talk' (p. 35), the examples also contained some connecting-talk. For example, in 'A lesson on the properties of materials – heat insulation', the teacher said, 'So you think the red one will be best. Why do you think that?' Similarly, in 'A lesson on the properties of materials – floating and sinking', there was the occasion when the teacher asked for reasons for saying that one of the items will float (C: 'It'll float.' T: 'Why?'). Another occurs near the end: 'Now there's a problem! How do you explain that?'

In the next examples, you will notice other instances of connecting-talk. The first example, 'Food for thought', is with younger children and the second example, 'Seeing the light', is with older children. (You may find it useful to underline the connecting talk.)

Food for thought

The teacher begins the lesson with tuning-talk, asking the children about what they like to eat and what they think food is for. He asks about pets and what pets eat and then draws attention to the birds that can be seen through the window.

T: 'Look at those birds. What do birds eat?'
C: 'Little bits of things in the dirt. Worms.'
T: 'Why do they eat worms?'
C: 'Because they like them.'
T: 'Just because they like them?'

C: 'It keeps them going. If they didn't eat anything, they would die. They're just like us.'

T: 'Yes, that's good. Has anyone seen birds eat anything else?'

C: 'Grass and bread and fat. We put fat out for the birds.'

T: 'Yes, good. You said they eat grass, John. Tell me about that.'

C: 'I've seen them on the grass. They eat the top bits.'

T: 'That's good. Can anyone tell me what the birds are eating on the top bits?' [No response.] 'Has anyone got a budgie?' [Some children respond.] 'What do they eat?'

C: 'Bird seed.'

T: 'Yes, they do. Look, here's some grass I brought to show you. Look at the top bits. Watch, I'll shake them. What's coming out?'

C: 'Bird seed?'

T: 'Yes, that's right, bird seed from the grass – grass seeds. What do you think of that, John?'

C: 'The birds are eating the bird seed on the grass.'

T: 'That's right. You have a budgie, Judith. Do budgies eat worms?'

C: 'No.'

T: 'Do all the wild birds out there eat worms?'

C: 'Some might like to eat seeds and nothing else.'

T: 'What if all the birds ate just worms? Would that be a good thing?'

C: 'No. They would eat them all up and then there'd be no worms left.'

T: 'What would happen then?'

C: 'All the birds would die.'

T: 'So, why is it a good thing that some birds eat seeds and other birds eat worms?'

C: 'It's good because there's something for everyone to eat.'

Much of this extract is about supporting mental connections by directing attention to what matters and by inviting thought about the relationships between the observations. For example, the teacher asked, 'Why do they eat worms?', 'Just because they like them?', 'What do you think of that, John?', 'What if all the birds ate just worms? Would that be a good thing?' and 'So, why is it a good thing that some birds eat seeds and other birds eat worms?' The teacher was keen to maintain contact with the children's existing knowledge by, for instance, drawing upon what they knew about pets and budgerigars, and relating that to the topic in hand.

Seeing the light

The teacher was teaching about light. She wanted the children to under-stand some simple effects that are a consequence of light travelling in straight lines. She showed the children pictures of car headlights and a searchlight on a foggy night then shone a small, powerful torch on a wall.

T: 'Look at the light on the wall. How does such a small torch make such a big circle of light?'

C: 'The light flares out when it comes out of the torch, like a car headlight.'

T: 'Show me what you mean.' [The child stands behind the torch and uses his hands to illustrate the edges of the light beam.] 'That sounds like a good idea. Let's use this piece of card and see if we can find the edge of the light.' [She takes a piece of card and holds it so it shows an edge of the beam of light. She moves it towards the wall, keeping the edge of the beam of light in view.] 'Does it flare out?' [The children say that it does. She has various children repeat this to find the edge above, below and on the other side of the beam.] 'It certainly looks like the light flares out. How can we be sure? Could we do anything to let us see the light flare out?'

C: 'Look at it on a foggy day.'

T: 'Yes, that would probably do it. It's not foggy today so we'll have to try something else. Look, I'll use the board duster and I'll blow some chalk dust into the light. How could that test our idea?'

C: 'The dust might show where the light is.'

T: 'OK. Here goes.' [She blows the dust into the light and the divergent beam becomes visible for a short time.] 'So, what did that show us?'

C: 'The light really does flare out.'

T: 'It certainly looked like it. Now then, I'm going to shine the light on the wall again. There it is, a big circle of light. Jane, hold your hand up in the light. Keep it still, please.' [Jane does so.] 'Look, there's the shadow of Jane's hand. The shadow is much bigger than Jane's hand. Why is it so big?' [Pause.]

C: 'The light flares out.'

T: 'I can see how that gives us a big circle of light but how does it make the shadow big?' [Pause.]

C: 'The light from the torch, it flares out past her hand, like this.' [The child demonstrates.] 'So it goes on the wall there. It can't go there because her hand is in the way.'

T: 'Yes, I think I see what you mean. Jane's arm is tired. Let's use this box instead of her hand. Now, show me where the light goes.' [The child indicates a straight line from the torch past the edge of the box to the corresponding edge of the shadow.] 'That's a good idea. Let's mark it with this piece of string.' [She attaches one end of string to the edge of the torch and stretches it past the edge of the box to the corresponding edge of the box's shadow on the wall where she fixes it in place.] 'Let's put other pieces of string on, all around the torch.' [The children comply and produce a net of straight strings that diverge from the torch, touch the edges of the box and end on the corresponding points of the box's shadow.] 'So, why is the shadow bigger than the box?'

C: 'Because the light flares out; it flares out past the box and keeps on going. There's a sort of hole behind the box where the light can't get. It gets bigger the further you go so it's big on the wall.'

T: 'Yes, I agree. What do you notice about all the strings?'

C: 'They're straight.'

T: 'What if it had gone like this?' [She gathers the strings on the wall together and holds them in her hand behind the box.]

C: 'The light would be getting behind the box.'

T: 'And what would happen to the shadow?'

C: 'It wouldn't be there. There wouldn't be a shadow.'

T: 'That's good. Well done! Suppose we wanted a small shadow, what should we do?'

C: 'Move the box near the wall.'

T: 'Yes, and why would that make the shadow small?'

C: 'The light wouldn't have flared out so much there.'

T: 'That's good. What if the light didn't go straight to the wall? What if it was all bendy? What would the shadow be like?'

C: 'It could be anything, any shape. It depends.'

T: 'Yes, that's right. But shadows are like this so light must go . . .?'

C: 'Straight to the wall.'

The teacher provided some preliminary experience of divergent beams of light (in pictures) so that the children had something relevant in mind. Immediately, she introduced the torchlight and asked for an explanation: 'How does such a small torch make such a big circle of light?' They had to connect what they now knew beams of light looked like with the effect on the wall. To make sure it was not a mere recitation of words, she had the child show her what he meant. To ensure the children understood the purpose of the chalk dust, she connected it to the fog they had seen in the pictures. The next step was to present the problem of the large shadow and ask for another connection: 'Why is it so big?' She focused attention on what mattered using concrete objects, namely, the strings. This highlighted the straight edge of the beam and demarcated the illuminated and shadow regions. With this in place, she could again ask for the connection to be made: 'So, why is the shadow bigger than the box?' The significance of the continuous straight edge was again highlighted by asking what would happen if it was not continuously straight or else was curved. The outcome is a connection between a cause (the way that light moves in straight lines) and an effect (the enlarged shadow). It is not, of course, a rigorous demonstration that light travels in straight lines. The teacher was more concerned to establish an understanding of what light travelling in straight lines means and of some consequences of that.

Planning your own connecting-talk

Have a go at planning some connecting-talk to prepare the children for one of the following lessons.

If your interest is in teaching younger children:

'What are those little bits, Miss?'

On a sunny day, the children notice 'little bits' floating around in the sunlight in the classroom. What are they? Are they germs? Where did they come from? What happens to them? You decide to use their interest and help them understand this natural phenomenon. Outline what you would do, what activities you might include and where you expect that connecting-talk could be beneficial. Illustrate what that connecting-talk would be. You should aim to bridge the children's understanding from something they know well to what they need to grasp that is new.

If your interest is in teaching older children:

Food chains

For the topic of *Food chains* (for example, grass is eaten by rabbits, rabbits are eaten by foxes), outline what you would do, what

activities you might include and where you expect that connecting-
talk could be beneficial. Illustrate what that connecting-talk would
be. You should aim to take the children's understanding from
something they know well to what they need to grasp that is new.

Monitoring-talk

You believe that the children have some grasp of a topic but you need
to know how strong that grasp is. For instance, when there was snow,
you took the opportunity to have a lesson on the freezing and melting
of water. The children examined snow crystals with a hand lens and
looked at cross-sections of the layer of snow in the playground. You
carefully scooped a shovelful of snow so that it was not compressed. The
children measured its depth and weighed it. They placed it in a bucket,
allowed it to melt, noted the depth of the meltwater and weighed it
again. Their talk suggests that they grasped the point of it all but you feel
you should check. 'So, why is the snow so deep?' you ask. They tell you
that a small amount of water can make millions of snowflakes. These pile
up deep with lots of air in between. You persist by asking them what they
mean by 'pile up deep with lots of air in between'. You ask them to tell
you something else that does this so you will understand what they
mean. One of them tells you that, 'It's like cornflakes!' You ask for
examples of situations when snow is more tightly packed. Responses
include reference to a snowball and the polished snow on the road after
cars have flattened it.

Monitoring-talk obliges the children to express or use their understanding so you can appraise it. If the children simply repeat what they
read or heard, they may be relying on memorization so it is better if
you have them use their own words. In the snow example above, the
monitoring-talk went further by asking the children for an analogy for
loosely packed snow (the cornflake response). You can also ask them to
think of other examples from their own experience and explain them.
Another useful test of understanding is to ask the children to make a
specific prediction ('So if it had been hailstones instead of snowflakes,
would it be as deep as the snow, deeper than the snow, or less deep than
the snow?') This is, of course, followed by 'Why?'

Interactions like this are also found in connecting-talk when it is
used to consolidate and extend understanding. Some talk can help the
children understand and, at the same time, let you know how the lesson

is going. The value of regular monitoring-talk is that it lets you know when things are going badly as or soon after it happens. You can then do something about it before the children become hopelessly lost. Monitoring-talk is not something that is confined to the end of a lesson; it is something you need to do as you go along.

Nevertheless, you need to know what the state of the children's learning is at the end of a session so that you can take it into account in planning the next unit of work. This means that you will need to give priority to monitoring-talk as you close a session. There is, however, a bonus. Having children express their thoughts probably makes them think more carefully and completely and, as well as letting you know something about the quality of their learning, it may also strengthen their understanding.

Accordingly, your oral interaction should seek to:

*   *Monitor and respond to learning.* This could occur at any point in a lesson although it may be more prominent in some parts than in others. The aim is to appraise the quality of learning and respond to it. Asking children simply to recall reasons and explanations may be a better indicator of memory than of understanding. Tasks that make children explain in their own words, use what they have learned in new situations and make predictions can provide better clues about the quality of learning.

In practice, tuning-talk, connecting-talk and monitoring-talk may not be completely separate in a lesson and just a few words can serve more than one purpose. Nevertheless, it is useful to think of them separately as it is a reminder that each has an important role and, at times, one of these roles may be dominant. Remember that the aim is to use whatever talk is appropriate at the time so that the children's thinking is moved forward smoothly.

Some monitoring-talk

In these lessons, the teachers used application in a new context to gain an insight into the quality of the children's learning. 'Sealed with care' is with younger children; 'A pithy tale of how to keep a cool head' is with older children.

Sealed with care

The teacher is teaching about caring for the environment. She has a large, stuffed, toy seal which she places on her lap. The seal tells her story to the children. It is about her life in the sea, what she does, what she eats, and the island where her baby seal waits for her to bring something to eat. 'Why do you think Baby Seal has to stay on the island?' asks the teacher. The responses centre on the young seal's vulnerability and inability to fend for herself in the water. The teacher is satisfied and the seal goes on to tell the children about the ship that sank and spilled oil into the water so that her eyes became so sore she could not see. For days, she had swum around not knowing where she was, becoming thinner and thinner because she could not catch fish. What had happened to Baby Seal? She did not know. When she did find her way to the island, Baby Seal was gone.

Having discussed the story and its 'message', the teacher had the children draw parallels with mess made on the school field by the painters who had spilled some paint.

T: 'Do you think it matters? Is spilled paint on the grass a good thing or a bad thing or does it not matter?'
C: 'The grass might die.'
C: 'Worms and things underneath might die.'
C: 'Birds might die.'
T: 'Why might they die?'
C: 'The grass can't grow with paint on it and then there's nothing for the worms and things to eat.'

This supplying of reasons in this new context is an indication of the extent to which the children have understood that the environment needs care.

A pithy tale of how to keep a cool head

The teacher had been teaching about keeping cool on a hot day. The teacher and the children contrasted sitting in a breeze and sitting in the shade. They distinguished between the possible effects of thin and thick clothing (for example, a thick and a thin cotton shirt) and between equally thick clothing that was made from different materials (for example, a satin-like blouse and a cotton blouse). They also thought that the colour of the fabric made a difference as one of the children recalled that her black dog soon became very warm when he stood in the sun.

The wearing of white clothes for sports in summer was also mentioned. Using a thermometer, plastic bottles of water, some fabrics, some poster paints, a shady corner, a breezy place and somewhere in full sun, they investigated the effect of shade, a breeze, fabric and colour on the rate at which heat was absorbed on a hot day. They found that all these made a difference. For instance, the black-painted bottles absorbed heat more quickly than the white-painted bottles, all else being equal.

In the teacher's store was an old, army 'pith' helmet, the kind worn by Royal Marines on ceremonial occasions. One boy said that he had seen explorers in a book wearing hats like that. Others agreed it was an 'explorer's' hat. The children had not discussed the hat before so the teacher used it to monitor their understanding. They would have to apply what they knew to explain its characteristics. Simply parroting words they had heard before would not do. Some of the teacher's monitoring-talk was:

T: 'Where were the explorers?'
C: 'Africa.'
T: 'Why would anyone want to wear a hat like this where it's hot?'
C: 'It keeps the sun off you. It shades your head.'
T: 'Yes, it would do that. This hat's rather special. Have a look at it.'
C: 'It's got a hole in the top.'
T: 'Yes. Why does it have a hole in the top?'
C: 'There's some little ones round the sides. I know! They'll let fresh air in and it'll go up past your head and out the top. Like a draught to keep you cool.'
T: 'Yes, that's very good. Is there anything else about the hat?'
C: 'It's white. That'll keep you cool because we saw that in the experiment.'
T: 'What did you see?'
C: 'The white bottle didn't get hot as quick as the black bottle. With the hat, your head's like the bottle.'
T: 'That's good. Do you think there is anything else special about the hat?'
C: 'Is it made of a special material that doesn't let the heat through very quickly?'
T: 'Well done! That's very good.'

The explanations the children gave for the various characteristics of the hat indicate the extent to which they understood how these properties affect the rate of heat absorption.

In both these examples, the application of understanding may provide you with an indication of the children's grasp of the topic but, at the same time, it may also help the children develop their understanding further. Monitoring-talk, therefore, is not just for your benefit.

Planning your own monitoring talk

Like most things in teaching, they generally go better if you are prepared. Try planning some monitoring-talk for one of the following:

- day and night
- the cause of shadows
- sources of light and reflectors of light
- the life cycle of a frog (frogspawn, tadpole, frog)
- the process of condensation
- checking that erosion is not confused with weathering

2.2 SCIENCE TALK AND PRACTICAL ACTIVITY

Practical activity has appeared in the examples earlier because it would be unrealistic to exclude it. Such direct experience has a lot of potential for supporting understanding but it is more likely to do that if you include some focused talk. This section looks more closely at how to do that.

Practical activity in science serves several ends. One is to help children learn attitudes, values, skills and processes associated with doing science. For instance, they learn to seek rational explanations and to appeal to observation and experiment. They also learn the importance of controlling variables in fair tests and practise reading instruments, such as a thermometer. Another end is to give children direct experience of what we want them to understand. It provides the raw material for their minds to work on. For example, we may want to illustrate that friction produces heat by having the children rub an eraser vigorously on paper and then lightly touch their noses with the eraser. Similarly, if we want them to grasp what we mean by the interdependency of living things, we may have them study life in a pond. In the same way, if we want them to distinguish between rocks, we may bring some into the classroom to be examined, tested and classified. Doing science like this to achieve such ends is a common expectation nowadays and, for many, is an inseparable part of science teaching. It is easy to forget, however, that the doing of practical work is a means to an end and we can do a lot to ensure it achieves that end.

The mental connections we want children to make are not necessarily obvious and they may be overlooked, misconstrued or interpreted in a different way. We are very capable of ignoring the bits and pieces of the world we do not understand. Merely having children engage in practical activity does not guarantee that particular connections will be grasped at all or as we had hoped. For example, children looking at twigs from different trees may fail to notice that some buds on the twigs are arranged opposite one another while others are dispersed along the twig and alternate. They see what we see yet do not notice the pattern. This is when talk is important.

Unlike some aids to learning, practical work provides direct experience and puts the task in the children's own hands, quite literally. At times, you will stand back and let them explore their ideas and make sense of things in their own way. When things go wrong, you may let the children persist for a while and intervene only when the work becomes so unproductive that it is frustrating and may be abandoned or becomes counterproductive and the children begin to develop or reinforce unwanted understandings. Even when practical work goes well, there still has to be some monitoring-talk if you are to know anything of the quality of the learning and take it further. The aim of science talk is to make the most of the activity and maximize understanding but it also depends on the kind of practical task you provide.

There are several kinds of practical activity. For example, there is the kind that extends a child's experience of the world. Suppose, for instance, you want to teach about soils. What exactly is soil? A first step could be to provide the children with a sample of soil which they examine with a magnifying glass. You could also give them a pair of tweezers which they use to sort the fragments. After this, you could provide a different kind of practical activity. For instance, you might point out that the task of sorting with tweezers is rather tedious and time consuming. How else could they do it? Eventually, you show them how to mix the soil with water, shake it in a transparent plastic bottle and let it settle. They examine the contents and find that the soil has been sorted. This activity, sometimes done as a demonstration, shows the children how to do something. It could of course, also develop an understanding of the topic. Another activity is the investigation or experiment. 'Is soil the same everywhere?' you ask. 'What is the soil like near those trees, in that hole and by the wall? Can they find out? Can they invent an experiment that will test the soils and see if they are different?' A problem like this is often intended to develop the children's grasp of the way a scientist works. At the same time, it could also support their understanding.

At times, practical activities may not fall neatly into one category. One may develop into another and they may serve more than one purpose. For instance, any one of the three kinds illustrated above could also develop practical skills, the first in using a magnifying glass, the second in observation, and the third in designing a fair test. Similarly, all could support an understanding of soils although the investigation, on this occasion, could be mainly to practise the construction of a fair test. In addition to the understanding of soils, there is also the understanding of the practical procedures used in the investigation. Why do we do it like that? What is the reason for that? To show how talk can support understanding, each of the activities described above will be treated separately.

Developing the children's experience of the world

Suppose you had to teach about plants and how plants do the things that they must do. Everyday experience does not usually teach a child how plants take up water (and the things dissolved in it). Instead, a teacher may provide that experience by, for instance, standing a leafy plant like celery in water coloured with a food dye. As time passes, coloured water is found to have passed up the plant's 'veins'. A cross-section of the stem shows the children the distribution of these 'veins'.

How can science talk help? Here is an example:

- 'Why did we colour the water?' (Looking for a reason, making a connection.)
- 'Can you see where the water is going? Show me.' (Directing attention.)
- 'If we leave it a long time, where do you think it will go?' (Asking for a prediction, requiring engagement.)
- 'Suppose we took it out of the water and cut it across, what do you think it will look like? Draw a picture to show what you think.' (Reformulating and translating ideas.)

With older children, this could be used to lead to an investigation. How, for instance, is the celery able to pull water up like that? Do the leaves have anything to do with it? Would anything change if we cut the leaves off? This could lead to a comparison of an intact piece of celery and one without leaves.

Prescriptive activity

This is when you have the child follow instructions more or less step by step. Perhaps you want to exemplify particular skills or processes or feel that the task is a complex one and needs to be structured for some of the children in the class. For instance, you decide to illustrate some changes in substances by baking some cakes. What will happen if we change the amount of baking powder? Without some experience of baking powder, the children's predictions may be no more than guesses. You provide that experience using beakers of water and spoonfuls of baking powder (another instance of an activity for developing experience of the world, as above). You continue:

- 'How can baking powder help cakes rise?' (Applying prior knowledge meaningfully.)
- 'What would cakes be like without baking powder?' (Asking for a prediction, requiring connections to be made.)
- 'What could happen if I put too much baking powder in the cake mix?' (Asking for a prediction, requiring connections to be made.)
- 'The recipe doesn't say how much baking powder to use. Can we do an experiment to find the best amount?' (Applying and developing learning.)
- 'What things should we keep the same?' (Applying and developing learning.)
- 'Why?' (Justification, providing evidence that there is understanding.)

During this process, you construct a plan of action on the board for the children to follow including instructions for making the cake mix. The children follow the recipe to produce mixes that vary in the amount of baking powder (Figure 2.1).

Figure 2.1 Increasing the amount of baking powder makes bigger cakes that, when lined up, serve as a pictorial graph

Investigations

These let the children practise their investigative skills in a less prescriptive way. For instance, in a topic about *Ourselves*, you could teach about the function of teeth, their specialized nature and causes of decay. You steer the science talk to the prevention of decay, teeth cleaning and what seems like exaggerated claims made by some toothpaste and toothbrush companies. Which is the best toothpaste and which is the best brush? Prior to the lesson, you stained some plastic or paper cups with tea, coffee or concentrated fruit juice by leaving some in each until it dries. You offer these as the test materials for toothpastes and brushes. (Initially, you may confine the children's attention to toothbrushes or toothpastes – one or the other – to simplify the task.) The children are asked to plan and carry out an investigation and prepare a report on what they find.

Before they do so, you have some discussion about what we mean by 'best' in the context of the investigation. As the children work, you discreetly observe, listen and monitor: 'That looks interesting. Tell me how you will do it?' 'Will that do what you want? Will it be fair to the other brushes?' 'Measuring the length of the amount of toothpaste to make them all the same; that's a good idea! I wonder if they will all be the same thickness? Oh, you've thought of that and they are. Well done!' As they plan their reports, you continue to monitor their thinking. 'How will you present what you have found out?' 'Are there any other ways you could show that?' 'If someone comes along when you aren't there and reads it, will they know what it means?' 'Can I tell you where I think they wouldn't understand?' 'Why do I think they wouldn't understand there?' The talk will probably, of course, be different for each group of children, assuming the groups work independently. There is, however, an assumption they may all consider. They did not test toothbrushes and toothpastes on their teeth but on cups. What do they think? Will their findings still be useful? Exchanges like these help to develop a scientific attitude by obliging children to think in particular ways, they direct attention to what matters and they help the children to process their ideas and produce a coherent, meaningful mental structure that we can call an understanding.

Prior knowledge and practical activity

There is a further matter to consider. If children have no prior knowledge to draw on, beginning with an investigation may not be the best strategy. They may not have noticed what you want them to investigate and they may lack a conceptual base for that investigation. Sometimes, children's out-of-school learning may be sufficient to provide some basis for an investigation. For instance, in a study of camouflage among animals, children may already know of the purpose of camouflaged clothing and camouflage paint on vehicles. This could be sufficient to lead into a study of animal camouflage. On the other hand, an independent, controlled investigation in the topic of energy may be less successful without some conceptual experience to begin with. Before embarking upon an investigation, your talk with the children should help you assess their existing knowledge and satisfy yourself that it is up to the task. If it is, then you could try going straight to an investigation.

If it is not, you may begin by developing the children's relevant experience of the topic with a prescriptive activity.

Practically talking

Some examples of talk being used to enhance the effect of practical activities follow. 'Gauging an understanding of evidence' is a lesson with younger children; 'Gauging an understanding of electricity' is a lesson with older children.

Gauging an understanding of evidence

The children have sorted a range of objects into groups: 'things that stretch' and 'things that do not stretch'.

T: 'So which things are stretchy?'
C: 'These things, Miss.'
T: 'How do you know that they are stretchy?'
C: 'Because we pulled them.'
T: 'How did that tell you if they are stretchy?'
C: 'Because, when we pulled them, see, they pulled out. They got bigger . . . long.'
T: 'That's good. What about this one? Do you think this will be stretchy?' [Teacher produces a plastic bag, not previously tested and unlike the items already tested.]
C: 'Hmm. Don't know. Maybe. It might.'
T: 'If I did this . . . [Teacher rolls it into a ball and compresses the ball.] . . . Would that tell us if it is stretchy?'
C: 'No! You have to do like this.' [Child demonstrates pulling action.]
T: 'Why do you have to do that?'
C: 'Because that pulls it. It makes it stretch. If it's not stretchy it won't.'
T: 'Show me.' [The child demonstrates and the bag tears.] 'That's all right. It doesn't matter. Did that tell us the bag was stretchy?'
C: 'It tore.'
T: 'Was it stretchy?'
C: 'It might have stretched a bit . . . but it tore.'
T: 'Which pile will you put it in?'
C: 'That one.' [The child points to the 'things that stretch' pile.].

This interaction raises a number of questions. For example:

- Does the child grasp the concept of evidence?
- Does the child grasp what counts as evidence of 'stretchiness'?
- Is the evidence of the child's thinking unambiguous?
- Is there a possibility that what the child would call 'stretchy' includes properties that the teacher would not call 'stretchy'?
- How might this teacher proceed?

It is apparent that this child knows what is meant by evidence. She refers to relevant, practical experience and, when offered an irrelevant version (compressing the bag), she rejects it and demonstrates what counts. Similarly, the child has some grasp of 'stretchiness' – getting bigger when pulled – but there may be some difficulties with where 'stretchiness' ends and 'tearing' begins. Is tearing a kind of stretching? The child may not be clear that it is due to a failure to stretch. In this respect, evidence of the child's thinking is not quite clear. The teacher might follow this with a direct exploration of elastic limit, where stretchiness ends and tearing, breaking or snapping begins. The children could benefit by being talked through an instance of stretching followed by tearing in which the stages are distinguished and named clearly.

Gauging an understanding of electricity

Following some introductory work on simple electrical circuits, a group of children are set the task of making a circuit that will sound a buzzer when a valuable ornament is lifted from its stand. The teacher attends to the work of other groups and returns to this one.

T: 'Is it done? Does it work?'
C: 'Yes.' [The children demonstrate.]
T: 'Oh, I like that! How did you do it?' [The children describe the physical arrangement of the materials.]
T: 'Oh, I see. How does it work? Show me where the electricity goes.' [The children trace the path of the electrical current.]
T: 'Now I understand. What would happen if that wire was loose?'
C: 'Nothing.'
T: 'It wouldn't work?'
C: 'Yes, it would still work.'
T: 'Why's that?'
C: 'Because, look, the electricity would still come from the battery, go through that wire and get to the buzzer, so it would buzz.'

T: 'Oh, so what's this wire for?' [Points to the wire from the other side of the buzzer to the battery.]

C: 'Nothing . . . like . . . we put it in because it's . . . it's always there.'

What did the teacher discover in the exchange and how might he proceed? This is another instance of a view of electrical current that is not like that of a scientist. The child probably thinks electricity is consumed by the buzzer in producing the sound so nothing is left to come out the other side (T: 'What would happen if that wire was loose?' C: 'Nothing'). One way of proceeding would be to have the child disconnect the wire he sees as irrelevant, note that the buzzer ceases to buzz, and have him try to explain it. This could then be followed with an analogy for the flow of electricity, such as that of water in a pipe, and hence the need for a complete circuit.

Using talk to support practical activity

Here are some lessons to do with that very variable material we call soil. As you read, think of the talk you would use to support the activity. You may find that jotting down your ideas helps you focus and develop your thoughts.

If your interest is in teaching younger children:

What is soil?

The aim of the lesson is to find out about soil, what it is, what is in it, and where it comes from. This is the sequence of events:

1   The teacher seeks to bring the children's existing knowledge about soil into their minds.

2   The children collect samples of soil from three different locations. They examine it with a magnifying glass and extract some of the different things they find.

3   The teacher points out that this way of sorting soil will take forever and asks for ideas of other ways they might sort the soil. They try sieving with only partial success. The teacher shows them how to sort soil by mixing it with water in a plastic

bottle, shaking it, then allowing it to settle. The children do this and compare their samples of soil.

4 Where have the different bits come from? A discussion ensues. They identify 'dead bits' and stones. The teacher has them put on safety spectacles from the design and technology corner and then hits two pieces of stone together over some paper. The children examine the bits on the paper. The lesson concludes with the making of 'soil' from sand, pebbles and humus. The children plant an onion in it.

If your interest is in teaching older children:

Can we make clay drain better?

The children learned from a farm visit that the farmer prefers a soil that has some drainage. The farmer had explained that too much drainage makes the soil dry while too little makes it soggy. A lot of the fields had clay soils. Clay does not let water through easily and some of the fields had water standing in pools on them. The farmer showed the children that the young wheat and turnips in these fields were rotting because of the standing water. Is it possible to make clay soils drain better and improve the fields? The aim of the lesson was to suggest reasonable ways of improving the drainage and then to compare them to find the most effective one. This is the sequence of events:

1 The teacher seeks to bring the children's existing knowledge about soils and what is meant by drainage into their minds.

2 The children compare the structure of soils that drain well with those that do not. Based on this, they make reasoned suggestions about what might make a clay soil drain more quickly.

3 The children design investigations that will compare the suggestions fairly.

4 The investigations are carried out and each group presents its findings, with evidence, to the other groups. The class discuss

the findings as a whole and make recommendations that the farmer might try. A report is written and sent to the farmer with their letter of thanks for the visit.

Practically talking

What would you do and what might be your focused talk in each of the following kinds of practical work? (You may assume that the children's prior knowledge is such that each kind of practical activity is appropriate.)

If your interest is in teaching younger children:

- Developing the children's experience
  Absorbency (sponges, wipes and kitchen paper).

- A more prescriptive activity
  How fast does grass grow? (You previously planted lawn seed in a tray of potting compost so that it is now about two or three centimetres high.)

- An investigation
  The most squashy thing I can find.

If your interest is in teaching older children:

- Developing the children's experience
  Erosion.

- A more prescriptive activity
  Can plants in the shade do anything about it? (You have previously planted a broad bean seed in a pot and it is now about three centimetres high.)

- An investigation
  Does water evaporate more quickly if you spread it out?

Monitoring-talk to gauge an understanding of an investigation

If your interest is in teaching younger children:

Snow time

There has been snow and the children bring snowballs into the classroom with them, hoping to keep them for the next break. The teacher asks what happens to snow and is told that it melts. 'What will happen if you leave snowballs in your coat pockets?' he asks. The children look uncomfortable and say they should take them out. The teacher takes the opportunity to have the children find out where snowballs melt the quickest. He asks for suggestions (with reasons). Will it be in a cup in a coat pocket, in a cup on a plate, in a cup in the refrigerator, or in a cup on the radiator? Their snowballs are used to find out.

The teacher needs to know:

- Do they understand what happens to snow?
- How well do the children grasp the problem?
- What is their grasp of the investigation (for instance, do they see the point of using snowballs of the same size)?
- How well do the children grasp the concept of drawing a conclusion that derives from their data and relates to the problem?

What would you advise? What specific questions relating to this context could the teacher try?

If your interest is in teaching older children:

The best wash

A teacher complains that there is paint on her handkerchief. The children suggest that she should wash it but she says that the last time this happened, the stain did not come out. Perhaps she did not wash it well enough. The outcome was that they suggested a variety of ways of washing the handkerchief. Which would be the best? The teacher put paint on a length of cotton cloth and cut it into strips which dry on the radiator while the children design an experiment to find the best way of washing the cloths. They then carry it out.

The teacher has several things to consider:

- How well do the children grasp the overall problem?
- Can they design a sound experiment that will solve the problem? Do they understand it?
- Can they distinguish between understanding a fair test and a blind application of a 'make all things equal' rule. How is she to gauge their understanding of a fair test?
- Can the children draw a relevant conclusion that derives from their data?

What would you advise? What specific questions relating to this context could the teacher try?

2.3 CHANGING MINDS

Your tuning-talk may have revealed understandings that are not appropriate. The children may change some of these fairly readily. For instance, some youngsters believe that water comes from walls, literally. Experience soon shows them that water in houses generally flows through pipes and these pipes bring it from somewhere else. Similarly, with older children, a belief that there is air on the moon is soon changed. However, some of these 'understandings' fit in with others that they have and work well in the children's limited world. For instance, it seems quite reasonable to believe that electricity flows to a bulb and is consumed there as it produces light. Everyday experience has taught us that we consume materials to get what we want: foodstuffs and fuels being notable examples. But here, common sense lets the children down. The scientist, Lewis Wolpert, once said that what is needed is not common sense but uncommon sense. The electricity is not consumed in the bulb – what goes in one end comes out the other – instead, it makes the thin filament hot as it passes through. Another source of inappropriate theories of the world stem from repeated exposure to false examples. For instance, many young children believe that if we blow up balloons with our breath, they will float away. After all, that is what is depicted in Winnie the Pooh books, and others. Changing children's minds about things like this may take time, new experiences, and a lot of talk.

The children's responses during tuning-talk can reveal how they understand things. We may start the process of change with a physical demonstration which highlights that there are problems with their view of things. We could have them predict what will happen then show them it does not work out like that in practice. For instance, we might ask children what it is like 'under the ground'. Having elicited their beliefs, we show them the new hole in the playground that the builders have made and have them contrast what they see with what they said. We follow it with a videotape and pictures that show what it is like at greater depths. The discussion would explore what these show.

At times, direct experience is not possible. For instance, if a child believes that anything will float if only the water is deep enough, this is difficult to confront with a counter-example. The answer is always, 'It needs to be deeper.' Even when you can provide children with a counter-example, that alone may not be sufficient to ensure that they look at things in a new light. We may also have to accept that children may not abandon their own theories altogether so that their old ideas coexist with the new ones. For instance, children will often believe that anything with air in it will float. This works reasonably well in a child's life. When you confront the idea with a sealed bottle that sinks, they can simply record this as one interesting exception to the rule. When you teach that it is 'lightness for its size' that counts, this may be established first as the rule to use in science lessons when you must. We should aim to strengthen the new ideas and show them to be superior. This is where connecting-talk can help a lot.

The point is that practical activity needs to be supported very carefully when confronting misconceptions or alternative ways of seeing the world. Unaided, children are not as likely to 'discover' other ways of looking at things as some like to think. It is even possible for the activity to reinforce these unwanted understandings. Similarly, group discussions can reinforce and even disseminate such understandings. Connecting-talk is needed to lead them away from one view and into another.

Being converted

Here are some examples. 'Air' is with younger children; 'Electricity' is with older children.

Air

In a lesson on air, the teacher had the children feel its presence around them by waving their hands and then by waving table tennis bats. The teacher now showed them some plastic bags and warned them that they should never put them on their heads. Under close supervision, the children then caught air in the bags and closed them to resemble balloons. The teacher asked what would happen if they let them go. The children expected them to float away but the balloons fell to the floor. The teacher continued:

T: 'What did you think would happen?'
C: 'I thought it would float right up to the ceiling.'
T: 'What happened instead?'
C: 'It fell with a bump!'
T: 'Why's that do you think?'
C: 'It's too heavy.' [Another child intervenes.]
C: 'You have to blow it up, then it floats.'
T: 'Why don't you try it?' [The child does so and finds that the bag still falls to the floor. The teacher takes a book off the shelf.]

T: 'Look at this. See Winnie the Pooh floating away. Well, what do you think of that now?'

C: 'It's silly. It's just a story.'

Here, the teacher had the children make a prediction based on their current understanding and encouraged them to test and reject it when they found it wanting.

Electricity

Faced with a belief that light bulbs consume electricity, this teacher introduced an analogy into the connecting-talk.

T: 'Think of electricity as water. If water flowed into one end of a pipe and made a waterwheel spin in it, would the water stop then?'

C: 'No. It would have to go on, out the other end.'

T: 'Right. Now electricity is a bit like that. It flows in here and . . .?'

C: 'Goes up to the bulb, makes the bulb work.'

T: 'And?'

C: 'Goes on through this one back to the battery.'

T: 'Right. That's good. Now electricity isn't exactly like water but it helps sometimes if we think of it like that. How is it different?'

C: 'It's wet.'

T: 'Yes, but what about this? If I cut a water pipe, what happens?'

C: 'Oh, you mean water runs out. Electricity doesn't do that.'

This is when your collection of books is helpful. They can prepare you with teaching ideas that can make changing minds a little easier. In theory, children could have an infinite number of unhelpful understandings but, in practice, some of their understandings are common.

Using talk to help change minds

Here are some examples of understandings children might bring with them. Some may be easier to change than others. Take one or two from each group and think through how you would help children adjust their views.

Too much or too little discrimination

- The term *animals* does not include people and insects.
- The term *plants* does not include trees.
- Wild animals are dangerous.
- The term *materials* refers only to fabrics.
- Dissolving substances, such as sugar in water, is described as melting.

Views of how the world works

- A person's body is much the same all the way through, rather like a cucumber.
- The world is flat.
- The sun moves across the sky.
- Looking is the process in which something is emitted by the eyes.
- The weight of something increases as its height above the ground increases.

2.4 PRESSING FOR UNDERSTANDING

Tuning, connecting and monitoring are some important kinds of focused talk that can develop an understanding of a topic. In addition, there is a way of using such talk which makes it clear that understanding matters and, at the same time, makes the children work at it and with it. This is a press for understanding. A press for understanding:

- obliges children to engage mentally with a topic for the purpose of constructing an understanding of it, and
- is persistent and insistent in that it occurs frequently and is reluctant to let learners escape easily from its demands.

This does not mean that the talk must be quick-fire and rapid-response. At times, that might be appropriate but an insistence on an instant answer can curtail children's thought. The result is that they respond with your words and your thoughts, not their own. Explanations can take time to construct, especially when children are thinking with fledgling understandings.

How much time should you allow for children to make connections and formulate a response? You do not want the time to be too short for reflection or so long that the children lose interest and look for other entertainment. Research suggest that four seconds should be sufficient but this cannot be a hard and fast rule. However, if you say to yourself, 1000, 2000, 3000, 4000, it will give you about a four-second delay before asking someone to respond. When producing an explanation, thoughts may continue to develop as we talk so, after a response, you could try simply nodding and waiting expectantly. Sometimes the child will extend the explanation or another will pick it up and add to it. Asking a child to explain another child's response to you is a useful strategy that supports understanding. It also maintains your press for understanding and encourages continuous attention from those not involved in the original response. In short, the aim now is to use tuning, connecting and monitoring-talk persistently and insistently but in a way that allows the children time to think, construct, reflect on and articulate their understandings. As a result, the children will learn that understanding and the thoughtful, reasoned response matter in your classroom.

Pressing for understanding?

In these examples, 'A roof over The Three Pigs' heads' relates to work with younger children, while 'The hardness of rocks' is to do with work for older children.

A roof over The Three Pigs' heads

Two teachers, Stephanie and Steve, are working with classes of younger children in the same school. They have listened to the story of The Three Pigs and are making houses in design and technology that no amount of huffing and puffing by the Big Bad Wolf could blow down. But what of their roofs? What if they rain in? What would be the best material for a roof? This is something that is explored further in science. These teachers' lessons were similar in many ways but there are some differences in the interaction. Who made the greater press for understanding? How was this achieved? What opportunities for different kinds of understanding are provided in these interactions? Bearing these questions in mind, you may find it useful to underline relevant talk in each extract or add notes in the margin.

Stephanie

T: 'Those houses look good. The Big Bad Wolf will never be able to blow those down. Which is the strongest? How did you make it strong so the Big Bad Wolf could not come along and blow the house down?'

C: 'I put in some lollipop sticks.'

T: 'Oh, that's a good idea.' [The teacher turns to another child.] 'How did you do yours?'

C: 'I glued those boxes in. I'm going to make them into beds.'

T: 'That's really good. Well done!'

Steve

T: 'Well, I think you are making some really strong houses. What makes your house strong?'

C: 'Those bits there. We glued them in hard.'

T: 'Did you? How do they make it strong?'

C: 'Hmmm, they . . . because they're not bendy.'

T: [Teacher turns to the partner.] 'How does not being bendy help?'

C: 'Because it keeps the walls up. They won't bend down if you push them.'

T: 'That's good. Why do we want our houses to be strong?'

C: 'So the Big Bad Wolf won't be able to blow them down.'

T: 'Yes. What will blowing do to that wall?'

C: 'Push it. Push it like this.'

T: 'Yes, it will. What blows at the walls of your house at home like that?'

C: 'The wind.'

T: 'Oh dear, I've just thought of something! What if it rains?'

C: 'I haven't put the roof on yet.'

T: 'Is this what you are going to use for the roof? Do you think it will keep the rain out?'

C: 'Yes.'

T: 'Why will it keep the rain out.'

C: 'Because it's plastic. Plastic keeps rain out.'

T: [Turns to the partner.] 'Do you know anything else you could use to keep the rain out?'

All else being equal, Steve made the greater press. For instance, he pressed for reasons and did not simply accept the child's indication that bits glued in make the wall strong. He wanted to know why they would make the wall strong. He also expected the child's partner to think and respond and he reflected some responses to her. Stephanie reduced the effect of her press because she failed to follow up the responses in this way. Kinds of understanding involved in this example are, for instance, conceptual (bendy, stiff) and causal (why the wall is stronger).

The hardness of rocks

These three teachers are talking about the hardness of rocks. You will find that the level of interaction is different in each. One of the differences is in the intensity of the demand for 'hard' thinking. Who made the greatest demand? How was this achieved? What opportunities for different kinds of understanding are provided in these interactions? Bearing these questions in mind, you may find it useful to underline relevant talk in each extract or add notes in the margin.

Janice

T: 'Now, children, look at these. I've got five different stones. They're all different. What I want you to do is think of an experiment to find out which is the hardest. Work in pairs. One person from each pair form a queue here and I'll give you some stones. When you finish, write about what you did in your science books. Remember how we do that? I've put a list of titles on the board to remind you. Everyone know what you've got to do? OK, let's get started.'

Andrew

T: 'Now, children, what's this? [Pause.] Yes, Kathryn?'

C: 'A stone.'

T: 'Yes, it is. Here are some more stones. Are they all the same? [Pause.] Yes, John?'

C: 'No.'

T: 'Good, that's right. They're different. Look, some are harder than others.' [He strikes another rock with them, taking care that bits do not fly towards the children.] 'Do you think you could find out which is the hardest? [Pause.] Could you, Sophie?'

C: 'Yes, I think so.'

T: 'Good. What I want you to do is to work out how you will do it. When we invent an experiment, what should it be? [Pause.] Brian?'

C: 'A fair test.'

T: 'You remembered. Well done! OK. Work in pairs and plan your experiment. When you are ready, bring it to me and I'll give you some stones to try it out.'

Jayne

T: 'In the break you were standing next to the wall, weren't you? Did you notice what was along the bottom of the wall? [Pause.] Yes, Dawn?'

C: 'Bits of stone.'

T: 'That's right. Where do you think they came from? [Pause.] Louise?'

C: 'The wall?'

T: 'Yes, good. Why do you think that?'

C: 'Because the bits are the same colour as the wall stones.'

T: 'That's a good reason. Look, I've got two stones here.' [She holds them up and strikes them together.] 'What happens when I hit them? [Pause.] John?'

C: 'Em . . . bits broke off.'

T: 'Yes, good. Did you all see that? Look, I'll do it again. [She holds them up and strikes them together.] There! See the bits? [Pause.] Do all kinds of stone do that? [There are some uncertain responses.] Look, I've got two more. Are these the same? [The class say they are not.] Let's try them. [She holds them up and strikes them together.] Did any bits come off that time? Kevin?'

C: 'Just one or two.'

T: 'That's right, so, what's different about these two lots of stones? [Pause.] Peter?'

C: 'The first ones aren't as tough as those.'

T: 'Good. Why do you think the first ones aren't as tough as these?

C: 'Because more bits came off the first ones. They can't be as tough. The bits are not held together as much.'

T: 'Yes, that sounds right to me. Tough's a good word. Can anyone tell me another word we could use?' [She takes responses: 'Hard.' 'Firm.' 'Well stuck.' 'Not brittle.'] 'Now then, the wall, which of these stones would be better for building a new wall. [Pause] Ian?'

C: 'That one.'

T: 'Why do you think that?'

C: 'Because it wouldn't wear away fast. The wall would last longer.'

T: 'Good. That makes sense. Suppose we had to choose stone to build a wall, what would you choose? [Pause.] Amanda?'

C: 'Choose a hard one.'

T: 'Yes, but how would you know it was hard?'

C: 'I'd bash them together.'

T: 'That's a good start. Is it a good test? [Pause.] Hazel?'

C: 'No. It should be fair. I think I would have to test it properly. Maybe drop something on it. Keep the heights the same.'

T: 'Yes. That sounds a good idea. [Pause.] Why are some stones harder than others? [Pause.] What's your idea, Alan?'

C: 'Er . . . some stones are made from little bits sort of stuck together. Others, well you just can't see the little bits, they're so well stuck in.'

T: 'That's sounds like a good idea. Ben, will you explain that for me, please?' [Ben does so.] 'Can anyone think of another one?' [There is discussion of various ideas and a decision that Alan's has some plausibility.] 'If I was to give Alan these stones, do you think he could tell us which was the hardest just by looking at them? [Pause.] Jane?'

C: 'Maybe, with a magnifier.'

T: 'Thank you, Jane. How would that help?'

C: 'It would let you see if the bits were stuck together well. If you couldn't see separate bits, it might be hard.'

T: 'Does that sound OK, everyone? Well, we have magnifiers. Let's give it a try.' [The class do so and sort the stones into those where the bits are visible and those where they are not.] 'So this is what we *think* is the hardest. Let's see if it really is. Do you remember what Amanda said about testing it?'

Jayne's talk with the class showed the most press for understanding. Notice how she asked children to justify their responses rationally. She also indicated aloud to the children the kind of response she accepts with statements such as 'Good. That makes sense.' Janice's talk was cursory, amounting to little more than telling the children what to do. Andrew asked some questions but failed to pursue responses. For instance, he asked Sophie if she could find out which was the hardest. When she said that she could, he accepted it without further comment. A task like this might involve, for instance, the development of vocabulary and the grasp of the concept of hardness, a descriptive understanding of some differences between rocks, a causal understanding of what it is that makes rock hard, and an understanding of the procedures involved in the testing of the rocks. Jayne's interaction with the children was also the longest, largely due to the extra questions she asked. The length of the interaction alone is not necessarily an indicator of its quality: what counts is what is said, not how much. In practice, however, you may find that there is more talk when you press for understanding because you are asking for more responses.

Hard pressed

If your interest is in teaching younger children:

Shadows

The children have done no formal work on shadows before but they know what the word means. You plan to have them understand that a shadow is caused by an obstruction to the passage of light.

- Give some examples of tuning-talk, connecting-talk and monitoring-talk for this topic.

- How you would press for understanding in this topic?

If your interest is in teaching older children:

Health

The children need to do some work on the effect of smoking tobacco on health. This is a new topic and their existing knowledge of the subject is fairly small.

•   What understandings would you want them to develop?

•   Give some examples of tuning-talk, connecting-talk and monitoring-talk for this topic.

•   How you would press for understanding in this topic?

Tuning-talk

Connecting-talk

Monitoring-talk

2.5 CUMULATIVE SUMMARY

This part has introduced key types of focused talk to consider when supporting understanding in science. These are tuning-talk, connecting-talk and monitoring-talk. The first aims to focus attention and bring to mind what children already know that is relevant and, if necessary, develop it. The second is about making sense of the topic, linking it with prior knowledge and making important connections within it. The third is about checking the progress and quality of learning. In a lesson, these kinds of focused talk may overlap or serve more than one purpose. A press for understanding persistently engages the child in constructing and expressing an understanding and in justifying it. It is intended to oblige the child to focus on understandings and let them know that you value them in science.

At this stage, the overall aim is to help the children form the understandings you target and you will generally tend to control the talk. The understanding that results, however, could be relatively insecure or otherwise insufficient. Opportunities to express that understanding in a less constrained way are needed. How to provide these is described in the final part but, before that, some strategies for supporting your focused talk are provided. Figure 2.2 brings together the first two steps for fostering talking sense in science.

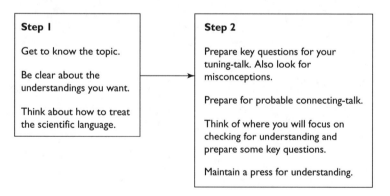

Figure 2.2 Summary chart

Part 3

Doing more for understanding

Part 2 was about helping children develop an understanding in science. It included some discussion of focused talk in practical activity and how practical activity can be seen as an aid to understanding. There are other strategies and devices that aid understanding and this part describes and illustrates some of them. They should make your support for understanding stronger. Some of these, such as bridging, relate to the way you present the science that is to be understood. They can make your talk more effective. Others, such as the book or videotape, can be thought of as an extra teacher in the classroom. They can add variety to your teaching but are, of course, blind and deaf to incomprehension. Talk, however, can make them more effective. How to use such devices and strategies to support your talk and how to use talk to support your teaching aids is illustrated. In places, some dialogue is used in the examples. Once again, *T* indicates the teacher's talk while *C* indicates the children's talk.

3.1 BUILDING BRIDGES

Sometimes, the gap between what the children know and what you want them to know is large and difficult to cross. Bridging helps them span the gap. If necessary, it provides small and manageable steps that help the children make the mental connections. For example, you may recall the series of steps used to teach children the meaning of pattern in science in Part 1. It began with the use of the word *pattern* in a context that is likely to be familiar to the children. After five steps, it ended with examples of pattern as regularity in nature. Going directly to patterns as regularities in nature may be too large a step for children to take if you want them to understand. The intervening steps are intended to establish and maintain links that will give the target meaning. Bridges can also be made using an analogy, provided the basis of the analogy is well known to the child or you are prepared to make it well known. For instance, parallels can be drawn between water flowing through a pipe and an electrical current flowing through a wire. Of course, analogies are seldom perfect so you will need to point out the imperfections to the children otherwise they may build them into their understandings. For instance, water can flow from a broken pipe but electrical current does not generally flow from the end of a broken wire. Here are some examples of bridging. 'Built like houses' is with younger children and 'Steamy scenes' is with older children.

Bridging to the process of melting

Built like houses

The aim is for the children to understand melting as a change that can be reversed and does not materially alter the substance. You could go straight to it and have the children watch ice or chocolate melt on a saucer on a warm radiator and talk about what they see. On the other hand, you could build in an analogy as a bridge to understanding. You could show the children a house made from plastic bricks. The press-stud connections between the bricks are strong enough to hold them together so the house keeps its shape, whichever way you turn it. You then pull the house apart, breaking it into smaller pieces. You place these pieces in a pile on a table as you break them off the house. Inevitably, as the pile grows, the loose pieces roll down, spread out and make a 'pool' of house bits. Now you have the children watch chocolate melt. You make connections between the house being broken into chunks and producing a 'pool' and the way the chocolate's bits are breaking away and forming a pool. The liquid is still chocolate but its bits are now loose whereas, before, they were joined together. With the house, it was you that broke the bits off. With the chocolate, the heat did it. If they let the chocolate cool, the bits will join together again. This is not the same as the house. No matter how long we leave it, the bits will not join together by themselves. Someone would have to do it – just like you are doing now for the children. So it went from house to bits to house again. The chocolate started hard then melted on the radiator and went hard again when it cooled.

The analogy provides something concrete and familiar to think with. It helps the children bridge the gap between what they know or can grasp readily and what they do not know.

Bridging to the process of evaporation

Steamy scenes

The aim is for the children to understand the process of evaporation and how it can lead to drying. You could begin with a wet towel and talk with the class about what happens to the water in it if it is left to dry. Alternatively, you could bridge their learning with smaller steps. Of course, you could still begin with the wet towel but this time you could use it to present the problem of what happens to the water in it when it is hung on the washing line to dry. At this point, you put the towel aside and take a dish of warm water. If this is stood outside on a cold day or in a cold place, the vapour leaving the surface of the water is often visible. Next, with the dish of water placed next to a cold window, the vapour will form a film of water on the glass, even if the water is cool by this time. The children are given time to convince themselves that what is on the window is water and that it has come from the dish. As you might expect, this would involve discussion. The wet towel is now held near the cold window and the children observe the film of water that forms on the glass. You invite them to explain where it has come from and what is happening to the water in the towel. The towel is then hung outside and, if it is a cold, bright day, the water vapour leaving the towel will be visible. (The vapour can also be made visible if it is placed in the open doorway of a cold refrigerator.)

This bridge has involved several steps, each one taking the children a little nearer to the target understanding. Each step aimed to give the children something to tie the next step to.

Constructing a bridge

Try bridge building for yourself. Choose a topic from the list below and construct a bridge between something the children will know well (or something they will readily grasp) and the target topic.

- being healthy
- life cycles
- animal skeletons
- friction between two solid surfaces
- conduction of heat

3.2   SCIENCE TALK AND SCAFFOLDING

When children attempt a task, they may falter or stall. Scaffolding is when you provide support at these times so that difficulties are overcome and understanding develops. One of the roles of science talk is to scaffold children's thinking. Scaffolding, however, is not something you provide continually. You do not scaffold a child's thinking to the same degree every time. On successive occasions, the amount of support is progressively withdrawn. In effect, the child is gently pressed into doing the parts you once helped them with so that they become able to do the task unaided. When that happens, of course, you will probably move on to something else and scaffolding may be needed again.

Some scaffolding

Here are some examples of teachers scaffolding children's thought. In 'Taking temperatures', a younger child's thinking is scaffolded; in 'Lights out', the same is done for an older child.

Taking temperatures

The teacher had some young children read the temperature every day on a thermometer scale marked in whole units. The children were expected to record the result on a large chart on the wall. This amounted to drawing a vertical red line to represent the red thread of liquid in the thermometer. One child showed she was unable to do this and the teacher attempted to scaffold her thought. Particular examples of scaffolding are shown in italics. The numbers in parentheses are referred to at the end.

T: 'Where do you think the line should go, Susan?'
C: 'There.' [The child correctly pointing to the name of the day on the chart.]
T: 'That's right. *What do we do next?*'   (1)
C: 'Draw a line.'
T: 'Yes, good. *Where will we start our line?*' [The child points to the name of the day on the horizontal line.] 'Yes, that's good. Now, where will it go to?' [The child is silent.] 'This is a tough one. We'd better work it out together. Now then, *what was the temperature number today?*'
C: 'Twenty.'

T: '*So the red line in the thermometer went up to . . . ?*'   (2)

C: 'Number 20.'

T: '*Can you draw me a red line like the one in the thermometer?*' [The child nods.]

T: 'Draw me what it looks like in the thermometer. *Where will you start?*' [The child places a red marker on the horizontal line next to today's name.]

T: 'That's right. Now then, draw me the thermometer line, *just like the real one. Which way will it go?*'

C: 'Up.'

T: 'Yes, good. *Now how far will it go up?*' [The child draws a relatively short line, roughly equal to the length of thread in the real thermometer.]   (3)

T: 'Ah! I see! Do you remember when we used the magnifiers? What did they do?'

C: 'Made everything big.'

T: 'Well, that's what we do here. *We make everything big so that everyone can see it.*' [The child stares at the chart then extends the line a little.]

T: 'That's better. *Do you think it's big enough?* [Pause.] *Look at our thermometer.*' [The teacher points to the one drawn on the vertical axis. The child stares at it.] '*Where've you seen these numbers before?*'

C: 'Thermometer.'

T: '*So where is our temperature, today?*'

C: 'There.' [The child indicates correctly.]

T: '*Here's our piece of red string. How do we get the length right?*' [The child holds the string along the length of the thermometer picture.]

T: '*So how long should our line be?*' [The child extends the string to the figure 20.] 'Good. *So that's how long our line should be. Take it to today. I'll help. There! Now what?*'

C: 'Draw the line.'

T: 'Well done. That's good. Now then, you tell me again how we know the red line should go up to there.'

The teacher was trying to find the underlying cause of the child's difficulty so was avoiding simply telling the child what to do. (1) is an instance where the teacher was scaffolding the child's thinking by helping her to be systematic and order her thinking. (2) is where the teacher was directing attention to the line in the thermometer. This line is to be reproduced on a larger scale. (3) is where the child revealed a difficulty. She drew the line the same length as that in the real thermometer and not up to the number 20 on the 'thermometer' scale. 'Just like the real one' was intended to have the child draw a vertical line but it was taken literally. The child may not have grasped the idea of drawing the thermometer thread to suit the picture of the thermometer rather than the real thing. Subsequently, the teacher attempted to establish the relationship between the two. It seems that more scaffolding may be needed on later occasions until this child has a better grasp of the idea.

Lights out

A child could not make his electrical circuit do what he wanted. The teacher responded by constraining and directing the child's thinking. This showed the child how to think systematically. Particular scaffolding is shown in italics. The numbers in parentheses are again referred to at the end.

T: 'Oh, dear! The bulb won't light up again. Now then, *what did we do when this happened last time?*' (1)

C: 'We looked at the bulb and things.'

T: 'OK. Yes, we did that. Let's get our thoughts sorted out so we don't waste time. *What should we check first?*' (2)

C: 'The bulb?'

T: 'Yes, we could start there. *Then what?*'

C: 'The batteries.'

T: '*How will you check them?*'

C: 'Try new ones.'

T: '*If they are all right, then what will you look for?*'

C: 'Hmmm . . .'

T: '*Well, if it's not a bulb or a battery, what have you got left?*'

C: 'Wires'

T: '*How will you check those?*'

C: 'Try new ones.'

T: '*Eventually, but what should you look for first?*' [The child is silent.] '*What would stop the electricity from going through all the wires?*'

C: 'When a wire is off . . . sort of not fastened on but it looks like it might be.'

T: 'Yes, that's right. *How does that stop things working?*' (3)

C: 'The electricity can't get past the break. Nothing happens.'

This may have been the first time the child had attempted to find a fault in a circuit himself. At (1), the teacher attempted to make the child's prior knowledge available. At (2), the teacher began the process of helping the child to be systematic. At (3), the teacher checked on understanding.

Scaffolding children's thinking

Here are some scenarios where scaffolding might help. The precise form of the scaffold, of course, depends on what the children say but you can, at least, plan how you would begin.

If your interest is in teaching younger children:

- The aim of the lesson is to show the children that leaves have things in common and have features that are different. The children are given a bag of leaves to sort. One child begins to place leaves in small piles, without regard to their characteristics.

- You show a picture of a mouse in leaf litter. You point out that the mouse lives in the wood and not in a house like them. In spite of that, it can keep warm, find food, know when the fox is near and hide. How can it do these things? What does it have that helps it? The response you receive is thin and largely irrelevant.

If your interest is in teaching older children:

- The teacher and class have been discussing the water system of a house and how hot water rises to a tank and can be stored there ready for use. Of course, it soon becomes cold unless the tank is lagged. What would be the best material with which to lag the tank? The children are asked to investigate the problem. One child looks at what others are doing and appears to imitate them rather than follow his own plan of action.

- The children have been doing some work on sources of light. They were given a set of pictures showing a mixture of sources and reflectors of light and were asked to identify the sources. The children tended to include reflectors among the true sources of light.

3.3 SCIENCE TALK AND MODELLING THINKING

So far, the emphasis has been on talk that helps us get the most from aids to learning. There is, however, another kind of science talk that can help children. This is when we describe our thoughts aloud for them, a process known as modelling. The aim is to let them know the kind of thought that counts and to exemplify how the children might go about their thinking. You may find that it is often easy to draw children into your 'think-aloud' talk.

Thinking into investigations

In the following examples, 'The problem with marking books . . .' is with younger children and 'A problem with the washing' is with older children.

The problem with marking books is that they are very heavy

'This bag of books is heavy. The handles are stretching. Are there other bags? Oh, there's some. There are one, two, three, four, five bags here. I wonder which is the best? I want one that doesn't stretch much. How can I find out? Now, let me see. I need somewhere safe to hang the bags. Let me see. I could fasten them on the backs of these chairs. No, I'd better not. If I put something heavy in the bags, it'll pull the chairs over and they might hurt someone. I know, I'll hang them on the coat hooks. There, they're ready. Now I'll put some books in them, the same number of books in this one . . . there, I've put the same number of books in them all. That's fair because they're all the same kind of books so each bag gets pulled down the same. The bags haven't stretched much. I'll put some more books in. They're starting to stretch now. Keep going. Oh, look, that one's really stretchy. This one isn't. That's really good. All you have to do is look at them and you can see which is the best.'

A problem with the washing

'Now, what we've got to do is find out which washing liquid is the best. Best. Hmm. That means which one gets things cleanest. What have I got? Let's see. There are four different washing liquids to test and this dirty piece of cloth to test them on. I'll cut the cloth into four, equal-sized strips. That means there's the same amount of cloth for each washing liquid. One liquid doesn't have more cleaning to do than another. I'll need four plastic bottles, one for each washing liquid. They need to be the same bottles. These are all the same so no one could say it was the bottles that made a difference. Right, what next? I'll need some water. Better put the same amount in each bottle so everything is the same for each washing liquid. Now I'll put in the washing liquids. Just a minute! I've heard that some people get a rash from washing liquids. I'll put on some plastic gloves. OK. How much should I put in? Oh, there's a spoon. I'll put a spoonful in each bottle. It's really gooey! I'd better be careful or it'll drip everywhere and then I won't have the same amount in each bottle. Right, now what? Put the strips of cloth in. Put the lids on. Now shake them. I'll do fifty shakes for each one to be fair. Then I'll let them stand for a minute and give them another fifty shakes. That's just like what a washing machine does. When I take them out, I'll dry them on the radiator and compare them.'

Modelling your thinking for the children

A topic for younger children: thinking through to a conclusion

Squashed: making sense of data

'We're finding out what to put in cushions! We have to find something that's squashy!' The children test several different materials by placing them on the floor at the same time and placing a brick on each one. What they see is shown in Figure 3.1. All piles of materials were the same thickness to begin with. As you examine the diagrams, think aloud to a conclusion. How would you encourage the children to join in with your thinking?

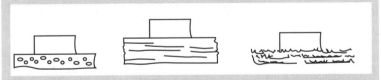

Figure 3.1 Left to right: brick on a thick piece of sponge, brick on a pile of cardboard squares, brick on a pile of carpet pieces

A topic for older children: thinking through to a conclusion:

Mopping up: making sense of data

The children found that some kinds of paper soaked up water better than others. 'It's the soft ones that are best!' said James. Ben was not so sure. He held some paper to the light. 'Some have small holes. It makes them sort of spongy. Maybe that helps.' They examined and tested various kinds of paper for water retention. The results are shown in Table 3.1. What do they suggest?

Table 3.1 Kinds of paper and the amount of water they retained

Kinds of paper	Amount of water retained
smooth, few holes	17 drops
furry, few holes	42 drops
smooth, lots of holes	36 drops
furry, lots of holes	61 drops

As you examine the results, think aloud to a conclusion. How would you encourage the children to join in with your thinking?

3.4   SCIENCE TALK AND PREDICTING

Asking children to make a rational prediction (not a guess) can be a powerful way of supporting understanding and it has appeared in some of the examples of focused talk. It can be so effective, however, that it deserves some specific attention. When we ask for a prediction, the children have to find a pattern in what they see or know and use it to predict the future. For instance, when children have examined different kinds of gloves, having them predict whether or not a pair of new gloves will be warm makes them look for a pattern to use. We want them to construct a relationship something like this: fluffy, soft gloves are warm; these are fluffy, soft gloves so they will be warm. To be sure it is not a guess, you would probably ask the children for their reasons; in other words, you would ask them to tell you the pattern or relationship they had constructed. You would probably follow that by having the children test their prediction. In this way, making a prediction can lead to practical work that tests it. This is the essence of a scientific investigation. For example, children may explore 'bounciness'. They use this experience to predict which of a set of balls will be the most bouncy and, of course, you have them justify their prediction. The next step could be for them to construct and carry out an investigation to test the prediction.

In order to make a rational prediction, children need something to guide their thinking. For example, when shining a beam of light on a mirror, where will the reflected spot of light be? If they know that the beam will 'bounce' off the mirror something like a ball from a wall, they could use that to predict where the reflected light will be. Faced with such a task, a child must either think through the problem and make a rational prediction or else make a blind guess. A blind guess probably does little for understanding. This is why it is useful to follow a prediction with 'Why?' The answer lets you know if the response has a rational basis. If not, you might model the process of making a prediction for the children to show them what it means. After that, you may need to scaffold their thinking from time to time. Used like this, asking for predictions is a part of your connecting-talk. At the same time, asking for a prediction is a way of checking for the presence of an under-standing. Being able to predict successfully and justify that prediction is an indication that the child has noticed a connection, seen a pattern or constructed a relationship that works. Children, however, sometimes respond with a guess. This is more likely when they lack experience or knowledge: they simply have nothing to work with to make a rational prediction. If this is the case, a solution is to develop or refresh relevant knowledge and experience. The following examples illustrate the use of predicting, first with younger children and then with older children.

A rational prediction or a guess?

Cut to the core

A teacher halves an apple, a pear, a grapefruit and a melon. The children examine the halves and remove and count the seeds. With the teacher, they discuss what these fruit seeds are for and what the purpose of the fleshy parts is. The teacher now shows them a fruit they have not seen before. Before she cuts it, she asks them what they think it will be like inside. They predict that it will have seeds in it and that they will be in the middle or in 'hollow bits'. The teacher proceeds to cut the fruit and the children examine the halves.

Is this a test of a rational prediction or a guess? The children have had some experience of what fruits are like inside. They know that there are seeds in all the fruits they examined, although some fruits had more seeds that others and the seeds in different fruits are different. They could, therefore, reasonably predict that this unknown fruit would contain hard seeds.

This does not, of course, mean that they will not guess. Some children may not use their experience to make a prediction. You could check on that by asking why they think there will be (or will not be) hard seeds inside the fruit. Of course, at this stage, the experience you have provided is relatively limited. Not all seeds are in the middle of a fruit. A tendency to over-generalize may be tempered by introducing a strawberry, which has its seeds on the outside.

Hard boiled

A group of children are given some hard-boiled sweets. They are asked to predict which will dissolve the fastest in their mouths. The children look at them and find they are very similar in appearance, apart from the colour. They like the look of the red one so they predict it will be the one to dissolve the fastest. They test this experimentally.

Is this likely to be a rational prediction or a guess? Would the investigation that followed be a test of a rational idea about what makes some sweets dissolve faster than others? If the sweets are similar, apart from colour, there seems no rational basis for predicting that a red one will dissolve faster than any other colour. On the face of it, it seems unlikely that they would find that any one sweet would dissolve faster than any other.

The lesson could be changed to give the children some rational basis for making a prediction. One way would be to offer a variety of sweets, some that crumble easily, some that are hard and some that are jelly-like, for instance. Talk could focus attention on the various properties of each kind of sweet and how likely it is that these would increase the rate at which it dissolves. Predictions could then be rational, scientific and testable.

Helping children make predictions

Choose one or two of the following questions and think about how you would support the children's thinking so that they make rational predictions. How would you check that their predictions are not blind guesses?

If your interest is in teaching younger children:

- Which hat will be best for keeping the sun off us?
- What will happen to the biscuits if we leave them in the oven too long?
- Will the poppy flower look like that tomorrow?

If your interest is in teaching older children:

- Which parachute will be the best?
- Which boat will go the fastest?
- What rock will be the hardest?

Monitoring understanding through prediction

Asking for a prediction is also a way of testing for understanding, provided you also ask for the reasons that underpin it.

Head to head

The children have been making simple electrical circuits using batteries, torch bulbs in holders and wires. You have described batteries as devices that make electricity go one way through the wires of the circuit. You now ask the children to predict what would happen if they were to connect two batteries in a circuit so that they faced one another (+ to +). One child says that they will 'Blow up'. Another says, 'Nothing'. How might you proceed?

3.5 SCIENCE TALK AND INANIMATE TEACHERS

Some things seem to offer to do the teaching for us. For instance, we switch on a videoplayer and show a tape with the title *Hot and Cold*. There is a commentator who talks about what the children see. The screen shows icicles and volcanoes, refrigerators and furnaces and a whole range of thermometers you could not possibly have in the classroom. What could be better? Showing the children these things is worthwhile and, assuming that the commentary has been well researched, what is said will probably be scientifically acceptable. But your children are unique. The commentator does not know them and the commentary was not written to suit their specific needs or your specific targets. You, on the other hand, do know them and have particular targets in mind. As you watch, you may see the children fidget and turn away as interest flags and comprehension breaks down. You see places where the key connections that you wanted the children to notice come and go. At the end, the experience seems less than it might have been. You need to take control of it, use what it has to offer and make it work better and, of course, you can do that through talk. What exactly does this mean?

As a part of your tuning-talk, before you play the tape, you could tell the children the title and ask them what they think the videotape will be about. Their ideas can be explored to stimulate the recall of relevant background knowledge. Another way of achieving a similar end is to take three key words from the topic, one by one, and ask the children to give you as many words (or sentences) as they can that relate to each one. They might then try to connect all the key words in a sentence. With older children, a third way is to give them a short test. This heightens their sensitivity to the things you tested when they watch the programme. Afterwards, you can give them the same test and boost their confidence when they see how much more they can do. Tuning-talk may also be used to give the children an overview of what they will see and draw their attention to the learning goals of the lesson.

When playing the videotape, you should stop it at places where there is a fairly natural break and check the children's grasp of the situation (monitoring-talk), and relate key points to examples that are familiar to them (connecting-talk). You can ask them to list up to three words they think were important in the part they saw. Reviewing these words will give you a feel for what the children think is the point of the lesson and you have a chance to put it right, if necessary, before the tape continues. Before continuing, you can ask the children to predict what the next part will be about. This returns their attention to the theme.

After showing the videotape, you need to know if the children have grasped the message. You may ask younger children to tell you about it or have older children write a summary of what they have learned (monitoring-talk). Another strategy is to work with the class as a group and construct a graphic organizer that captures the essentials of the topic (see also later). You could also set practical tasks or questions to answer that test understanding and the application of learning.

This does not, of course, apply only to videotapes. For instance, if you use a science book in the classroom, the temptation can be to let it get on with the task of teaching. Similarly, children sitting at a computer, using some science software, may be left to its teaching. We use such things because they can make a useful contribution to the lesson. Nevertheless, you need to use your monitoring-talk to check that they have been as effective as they appear and you may have to support them at times with tuning-talk and connecting-talk. Here are some examples. The first is talk to support a book for younger children. The second is talk to support a videotape shown to older children.

Assisting assistants

Rainforest animals

The children have been learning about *Caring for pets*. The teacher wants to widen the topic to include a concern for wild animals and develop some awareness of the difficulties that some of them have. Together, they look at books and see pictures of a variety of wild animals. These are sorted into animals that live here and animals that live elsewhere. An illustrated book about the plight of rainforest animals is introduced. It describes the animals' problems as people encroach on and destroy their habitat. An example of supporting talk is as follows.

Before reading the book to the children

- 'What do you think the story is going to be about?'
- 'What animals do you think will be in this book?'
- 'What do you think they do every day?'
- 'Where do they get their food? What do they eat?'
- 'Do you think it's easy for them to find food?'

During the story

- 'Have the birds got lots to eat?'
- 'What do you think the noise is that frightened the animals?'
- 'Look, it's a bulldozer! What do bulldozers do?'
- 'Why is taking the trees away bad for the birds?'

After the story

- 'Why were those birds so unhappy?'
- 'What will happen if all the trees in the forest are chopped down?'
- 'Does it matter if there are birds?'
- 'Should the people in the story have done something about it? What do you think they could do?'
- 'The people are poor and they have to make money to buy food. Is there anything you think they could do?'

Pond life

The aim of the lesson is to learn about the interdependence of living things as illustrated by food chains. The teacher decides to use a videotape on *Pond Life* to introduce the topic. Here is some talk intended to help the children gain more from watching the videotape.

Before playing the tape

- 'I'm going to show you a video called *Pond Life*. What do you think it's about?'
- 'What kinds of animals do you think you might see?'
- 'What do you think snails eat?'
- 'What kinds of plants might you see?'
  [The teacher issues a test sheet at this point.]
- 'Before we start, let's see how many of these questions you can answer. We'll try it again at the end to see how much you've learned.'

While showing the tape

- 'Look at that. What's it eating?
- 'Do you think it's safe in the pond? Is there anything that might eat it?'
- 'See all that pond weed. What are those little things on it?'

After showing the tape and now using the chalkboard

- 'Think about all the animals in the pond. Can you tell me one?'
- 'What does it eat?' [The teacher uses these to begin a food chain on the board.]
- 'Does anything eat it?'
- 'What do you think would happen if there was no pond weed in the pond?'
- 'Why do you think that?'
- 'What might happen if there were no frogs in the pond?'
- 'Why?'
  [The teacher draws their attention to the test sheet.]
- 'Let's try those questions now. I'll bet you'll be surprised by how much you've learned.'

Talk and inanimate teachers

Think of a book, videotape or computer program you use or could use in your science teaching. How might you support it so that the children gain more from it? Consider where you might stop the tape for talk. What would your talk be at those points?

Before using the teaching aid:

While using the teaching aid:

After using the teaching aid:

Is it possible to construct a simple diagram that collects together the information and ideas that the teaching aid presents? Try drawing such a diagram and mark on it the places where you may need to provide additional support for understanding.

3.6 SCIENCE TALK AND STORIES

Stories can also support understanding. They often describe events in the order in which they occurred and this makes them fairly easy to grasp. It is a common form of communication and children are familiar with the structure so it can be an effective way of providing the context for a problem or an explanation. It also seems to encourage children to participate in a discussion. As with other aids, however, you will probably have to plan the key parts of your talk before you start. To illustrate, here is a story. 'Scales of Justice' could be used to stimulate talk about fair tests. Some science talk you might use during or after reading the story is listed at the end.

Scales of Justice

'It's happened again!' shouted Housemouse. 'Every time I turn my back, someone eats all the biscuits!'

'Oh, do calm down', said Dormouse. 'What exactly do you mean, "someone eats all the biscuits"?'

'But, didn't you see, Dormouse? I put out a dozen biscuits. You took one, I took one, Vole took one, and', he paused, looking hard at Rat, 'Rat took one. And now there are none left!'

'Oh, really, Housemouse', said Rat, brushing crumbs from his coat. 'If I didn't know better, I'd say you were blaming me!'

'Hmmm', said Vole, staring at Rat. 'I may have been dozing but I might just have seen . . .'

'Oh, really, Vole!' said Rat. 'If you're going to talk like that, I'm going home.'

'Not so fast', said Housemouse, thinking he saw a little bit of guilt in the face of the escaping Rat. Grabbing him by the collar, he said, 'Onto the scales with you, Rat!'

Rat struggled but was made to stand on the scales.

'There!' said Housemouse. 'Just look at that! Five hundred grams! I'll bet two hundred of that's the biscuits you were too greedy to share.'

'No, it's not!' answered Rat, indignantly. 'I've got big bones so I weigh a lot. Always have.'

'Well, Housemouse', said Vole, 'I don't think you've settled things one way or the other. You'll have to do better than that if you're going to be fair to Rat.'

'Be fair!' muttered Housemouse, releasing Rat's collar. 'Be fair,' he grumbled. 'It happens every time we have tea.' All the same, he went to the cupboard for another packet of biscuits.

Dormouse poured everyone another cup of tea and they all took a biscuit from the new packet. Housemouse watched carefully. He thought he should put the packet back in the cupboard but that would make him seem mean so he left it on the plate. Soon, their conversation died away and the warmth of the fire made them sleepy. One by one, they dozed, even Housemouse who tried to keep his eyes open long after the others had closed theirs.

'It's happened again!' shouted Housemouse, making everyone jump.

'Dear me, Housemouse', said Vole, 'I'm getting too old to have frights like that. Do stop shouting.'

'But it's happened again', insisted Housemouse. 'All the biscuits have gone.'

'Oh, dear', said Dormouse, 'so they have.'

'On the scales!' demanded Housemouse, looking hard at Rat.

'I say, Housemouse, old chap. Do take it easy', said Dormouse.

'Yes, indeed!' said Rat, puffing out his chest. 'I find your accusations quite aggravating. Why, I could just pop you one on the nose!' Rat took off his waistcoat and threw it aside. 'Put 'em up, Housemouse!' he said. 'A chap can't just sit there and be accused, you know.'

'Now just sit down, both of you', said Vole, firmly. 'That's not the way to settle anything.' Housemouse and Rat did as they were told but glared at each other.

'Oh, Rat', said Dormouse, always willing to believe anyone. 'You can easily show Housemouse you didn't take the biscuits then I'm sure Housemouse will say he's sorry. Just step on the scales again!'

Rat reluctantly stepped on the scales.

'Five hundred grams!' he shouted, with, Vole thought, a little bit of surprise in his voice.

Housemouse stared at the scales and then at Rat.

'Oh, dear!' he said. 'I really am sorry, old friend. How could I ever have doubted you?'

'Yes, and you shouldn't have, but you did, didn't you?'

'That's enough', said Vole. 'Housemouse has apologized so let's all settle down again.'

So that's what they did and, by ten o'clock, they had all forgotten the case of the missing biscuits. Except for Vole, who glanced from time to time at Rat's waistcoat and thought about being fair. But, for the sake of peace and friendship, he said nothing.

How could you use such a story? Here are some questions you could ask:

- Who did Housemouse think had eaten most of the biscuits? (*Rat.*)
- What was he trying to show by weighing Rat? (*That Rat weighed more because he had eaten the biscuits.*)
- When Housemouse weighed Rat the first time, why was this not a good test to see if Rat had eaten most of the biscuits? (*Housemouse did not know what Rat weighed before. It needs a before and after weight to see if there has been a change.*)
- When Housemouse weighed Rat the second time, what did he find? (*Rat weighed the same.*)
- Did that show that Rat had not eaten the biscuits? (*No. It was not a fair test.*)
- Why was it not a fair test? (*Because Rat had taken his waistcoat off so things were not the same both times.*)
- How could he have made it a fair test? (*By making Rat put his waistcoat on.*)
- Suppose that Rat (and his waistcoat) had weighed more the second time, would they have been absolutely certain that Rat had eaten the biscuits? (*No. It would be evidence that Rat ate the biscuits but there could be another reason why he weighed more. Did he have lots of cups of tea?*)
- How could they have made it a better test? (*By making Rat wear his waistcoat and by adding the weight of the tea and his legitimately eaten biscuit to his first weight. An increase beyond that would be very suspicious if nothing else had changed.*)

Which of these questions you ask depends on the age and experience of the children. The last one, for instance, seeks a greater control of variables than the earlier question to do with making a fair test. Such questions could be asked during the story or all together at the end. If the children's memory for detail is limited, asking questions during the story may be the better approach. It also allows you to monitor understanding as the story progresses, reducing the chance that someone is left confused. You would, however, probably feel more comfortable when telling such a story if you have decided what the main questions will be beforehand. Making a note of them in the margins provides you with an effective prompt.

Teacher talk and stories

If your interest is in teaching younger children:

Here is a short story that might be used as a part of the support you could provide for young children to understand temperature. As you read it:

- think of your tuning-talk
- identify the parts of the story where you might pause for connecting-talk
- plan some monitoring-talk.

Thomas the Tiger Keeps Cool

Thomas the Tiger was in his hot, steamy forest on a hot, steamy day. He lay under a tree and felt hot and steamy.

'Oh, it's just too hot!' he said as he flicked an ear to make a fly buzz off. 'It's hot enough to make your claws go soft!'

He looked at his claws and wondered if claws really can go soft.

'What I need is somewhere cool!' so he slowly stood up and dragged his feet to the river. Usually, he would walk quickly but, he thought, he ought to be careful in case claws really do go soft.

When he reached the river, Thomas sat on the bank and dangled his paws in the cool water.

'Aaaah!' he said, with pleasure. But the river was not in the forest. There were no trees on the river bank. The sun beat down on his head until he thought his head would melt. In fact, he squeezed it a bit to make sure it was not just a bit soft. He stood up again and slowly dragged his feet back to the forest. Under a tree, he curled up in the shade and his head felt better. 'Aaaah!' he said, with pleasure.

After a while, he felt his paws becoming hot again.

'Oh, no!' he groaned. So he went back to the river and dangled them in the water. 'Aaaah!' he said, but soon, his head felt too hot, so he went back to the tree. Then he went back to the water, and back to the tree, and back to the water, and back to the tree. He became more and more unhappy all the time.

Helen the Hippo was wallowing in the stream, watching Thomas.

'What are you doing?' she asked.

'Melting', replied Thomas, glumly.

'Tigers don't melt', said Helen.

'Doesn't feel like it!' complained Thomas, irritated.

'Why don't you do something about it?' asked Helen.

'I am!' replied Thomas, sharply.

'It doesn't seem to be working', said Helen.

'Well, the trees are over there and the river is over here so there's nothing much I can do about it!'

'Yes', agreed Helen, 'but you could bring the part of the tree that matters over here.'

'Oh?' said Thomas.

'Tigers can climb trees, you know', added Helen.

Thomas stared at her then at the tree.

'Ohhhh!' he said. 'You mean . . .'

So Thomas went back to the tree and, even though he thought his claws had turned to rubber and his head to jelly, he climbed to the top of the tree. Choosing a big branch with lots of leaves on it, he bit it off and let it fall to the ground. He slid and slithered down the tree and picked up the branch. Tigers are very strong so it was no bother to carry it to the river bank. On the bank, he stuck the branch in the ground and his feet in the water. Sitting underneath his leafy sunshade, with his feet in the cool water, he thought to himself, 'Why didn't I think of that? Maybe that's what happens when your claws begin to melt and your head goes soft.'

If your interest is in teaching older children:

Here is a short story that might be used as a part of the support you could provide for some aspects of science relating to health and the human body. As you read it:

- think of your tuning-talk
- identify the parts of the story where you might pause for connecting-talk
- plan some monitoring-talk.

The Very Dirty Giant

You all know the story of Jack and the Beanstalk? Well, things did not really happen like that. You see, the newspaper bosses wanted a story so they could sell their papers. The Jack and the Beanstalk story was really nothing special so they changed it a bit and that is the one that got into all the books. This is what really happened.

Jack had this uncle who was a giant. Some people are just lucky like that. Anyway, he used to visit his uncle once a week. Once a week was enough because, in those days, giants always lived at the top of giant beanstalks. Jack's uncle did not like living at the top of a beanstalk. He hated heights and you must have noticed how beanstalks sway about in a breeze. But, what could he do? Everyone expected giants to live at the top of beanstalks so that's what he did. Jack didn't like it much either because climbing that beanstalk was hard work. That is why he visited his uncle only once a week.

Anyway, it all happened on a Wednesday. In those days, there were no schools to waste your time and Jack decided to visit his uncle. Up the beanstalk he went and his aunt, who was pleased to see him, asked him to stay for dinner. Jack's mother had told him never to stay for a meal but he was hungry so, why not?

'Fe, fi, fo, fum!' said the giant because that is what everyone expects giants to say.

'I smell the smoke from your bum!' said the giant's wife. Not everyone knows that's what giants' wives say.

'Where's my dinner?' complained the giant. In those days, men never made meals.

'On the table!' she said, slamming a huge pie on the table in front of him. The pie was as big as a bus and made the table groan and sag under its weight.

'Tuck in, Jack!' she said kindly, giving him a spoon.

'Yum!' said the giant, grinning from ear to ear and showing two rows of green teeth. 'I'll bet you're glad you came today, young Jack.' The giant poked his dirty fingers into the pie and sucked the gravy off them. 'Delicious', he announced, picking up his spoon. It was really a shovel but his wife called it a spoon when they had company. He shovelled up a great pile of steaming meat, fat, gristle, greasy gravy and pie crust. Just then, a fly landed on his nose.

'Achoooo!' bellowed the giant, sneezing stuff that ought to stay up his nose onto his shovelful of pie. The fly, which was also a giant, landed with a splat. It had a taste.

'Gerroff!' roared the giant, waving the shovel about. The fly had seen the giant eat flies so it did as it was told. The giant glared at it and shovelled more pie into his mouth.

'Arggh!' he shouted, as he bit some crust. He poked his dirty finger into his mouth and pulled out a piece of tooth.

'Serves you right!' said his wife. 'You never clean your teeth so what do you expect. And I bought you that new toothbrush', she added, pointing to a new broom standing in a pile of yesterday's slops.

The giant glared at her and ate very carefully with the teeth on the other side of his mouth. Jack did not know what to do. His teeth were fine. He could have tried maybe just one corner of that pie but now it was covered with things he did not want to think about.

'Come on, lad! Eat up!' said the giant.

'Yes, uncle', said Jack in a very quiet voice. He stuck his spoon in the pie and pulled it out. On the spoon was a . . . No! No! he thought, closing his eyes.

With his eyes tight shut, he took hold of the . . . thing, and pulled. It came out of the pie with a plop and fell on his plate.

'Oh, you've found a really yummy bit', said his uncle, spraying him with crumbs, gravy and fatty bits.

Jack opened his eyes and stared at the thing on his plate. It was a rat. To be fair, it was a well-cooked rat but, well, it was still a rat. Jack felt strange. Something was coming up from his stomach. He slapped his hand over his mouth and dashed out. He had never come down the beanstalk so fast in all his life.

Of course, the neighbours saw him tumbling, falling, tripping and being sick down the beanstalk. They saw his strange colour, too, and you know how neighbours talk. That is how the story started and then the newspaper people got hold of it. They said Jack chopped down the beanstalk but that's just not true. In fact, Jack's mother went to the council who sent someone out to talk with the giant and his wife. The giant had to have some teeth out but now he keeps what he has left bright and clean. And flies, large and small, are kept out of the house and dirt is swept out at least once a week. Jack's mother even gave them a giant bottle of disinfectant to kill the giant germs. And Jack still goes to see his aunt and uncle but, somehow, no matter how hard he tries, he just cannot get there in time for a meal.

3.7 SCIENCE TALK AND GAMES

Games that require the recall of facts are relatively easy to organize because valid play tends to be obvious to the children. For instance, a card that states 'The number of legs of a spider' is matched with the card that carries the figure 8. Matching it with a card that carries another figure would, let us hope, produce a flurry of disagreement. Such games may strengthen the recall of knowledge but probably have limited value when it comes to supporting a new understanding. Games that are more likely to support understanding could, for instance, call for moves that have to be justified. Whether to accept or reject the justification can produce lively debate as each player tries to ensure the others neither cheat nor secure an advantage through illegitimate moves.

You may use a game to bring relevant prior knowledge into the children's thoughts (like tuning-talk). This could be a place for a relatively simple, even factual game. For instance, near the beginning of a lesson, you could use a quick game to tune children's thinking to the task in hand. Suppose you want to develop the concept of transparency as a property of materials. First, you provide the children with dice. Two or more children sit in a group and take turns to throw a die. On a large piece of card are listed the tasks associated with each number, such as:

1	Think of one thing that lets light through	1 point
2	Think of two things that let light through	2 points
3	Think of three things that do not let light through	1 point
4	Have a rest!	0 points
5	Think of one use of things that let light through	1 point
6	Think of two uses of things that let light through	2 points

The children have to respond to the task that chance gives them when they throw the die. The same object cannot be referred to more than once. The winner is the one with the highest score.

You may have a game that obliges children to construct, express, translate or apply new relationships (like connecting-talk and monitoring-talk). Such a game is more likely to need your attendance, at least as the final appeal judge of what constitutes acceptable responses or moves. Suppose you have been teaching about electrical circuits and your aim was to teach the children about the need for a complete circuit. To consolidate or extend the children's understanding, you could prepare a set of playing cards with 'part-circuits' drawn on them, like those in Figure 3.2. The cards, when placed together could make a complete and

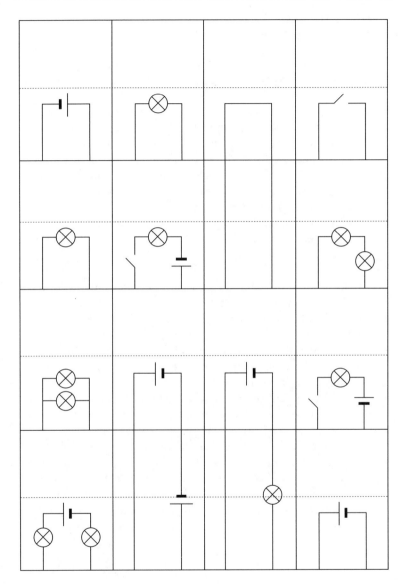

Figure 3.2 Cards for the electrical circuit game

satisfactory circuit or, at least, be on the way towards making one. The rules of such a game could be as follows:

1 Shuffle the cards and place the pile face down on the table.
2 Decide who is to go first. That person takes the top card from the pile and places it face up on the table.
3 The second person now takes a card and plays it, if possible. The play should either produce a complete and satisfactory circuit or be on the way to making one. If the player cannot make such a circuit, he or she misses a go and keeps the card to try to play it next time. If a satisfactory circuit is completed, that player collects one point and has another go. If, however, the circuit is unsatisfactory, the player removes the card, misses a go and loses a point.
4 The first person now takes a card and proceeds as in 3.
5 The play proceeds until no further play is possible. The player with the most points wins.

Note that, like dominoes, blank ends can be placed together as a go (but do not score points). There are two levels of difficulty. In the first level, side branching from the blank ends is allowed. This provides more opportunities to go. At the second level, no branching is allowed. An example of a part of a game is shown in Figure 3.3. (Players must guard against making circuits with batteries that oppose one another and cancel one another's effect.)

'Being like a scientist' can be a special kind of play or game for children. The tasks associated with scientific inquiry provide opportunities for this kind of 'game'. You may, of course, increase a sense of play-like engagement by presenting the task as a problem and inviting the children to deal with it by 'being a scientist'. Games and play in the classroom do not have to be frivolous or alter your routine unduly or lead to difficulties in class control. As with other classroom activities, you need a clear transition strategy that takes you efficiently from one activity to the next.

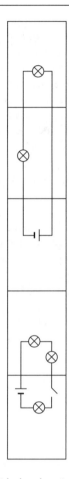

Figure 3.3 An example of play with the electrical circuit cards

Game time

Try inventing or adapting a game to support understanding for a science topic you will teach in the near future (or one taken from the list below). The game could be for use by one child or several children or could be a game that is led by you.

Some science topics to choose from (or choose one to suit what you will teach):

- Living, once-living, never lived (to practise applying criteria to sort living and non-living objects).
- Changes (to practise recognizing before and after the changes, including the cause of the change).
- Camouflage (later, you would draw on the understanding achieved when discussing the appearance of animals).
- The right one for the job (choosing materials that suit a purpose).

Some types of games you might consider are:

- a dice game
- a board game with counters, like Ludo or Snakes and Ladders
- a card game, like Snap (where the matching cards do not have the same pictures but represent instances of the same concept, pattern, or relationship)
- a word game, like a crossword.

How will your game support understanding?

3.8 SCIENCE TALK AND GRAPHIC ORGANIZERS

Holding a lot in your mind at once can make thinking difficult. A graphic organizer is a diagram which shows the connections or relationships between things. Such diagrams can behave like a memory extension and hold ideas and thoughts for us while we think about other things. This is particularly useful when we are trying to understand something new and we have a tenuous grasp on it. Building a diagram on the chalkboard with the children can help them structure and verbalize their thoughts (connecting-talk). It also reveals the quality and fluency of those thoughts (monitoring-talk).

Figure 3.4 shows a simple graphic organizer for the development of a flowering plant from a seed. In effect, it is a compact way of showing what happens over a relatively long period of time. However, the conventions in these diagrams have to be learned. For instance, children need to know that the seed, seedling and flowering plant are not all present at the same time, that the arrows mean NEXT, and that only three snapshots of a continuous event are shown. This is probably best done by talking through the diagram and then having the children do the same with this and similar pictures. It may help if you ask the children to draw intermediate stages that are not shown. For instance, what does the plant look like between the seedling stage and the flowering stage?

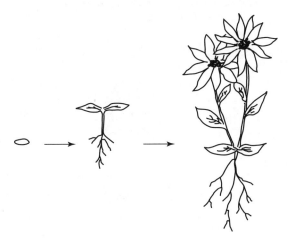

Figure 3.4 A graphic organizer showing the sequence: seed, seedling, flowering plant

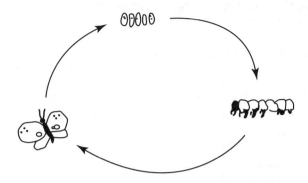

Figure 3.5 A graphic organizer showing the cycle: egg, caterpillar, butterfly, egg

Figure 3.5 depicts the life cycle of the butterfly. Again, the child needs to know the conventions. In this case, the arrows could be omitted and the child might be asked to supply them (monitoring-talk).

Graphically organized

Try designing a graphic organizer that highlights a scientific pattern or relationship in a topic you will have to teach in science (or choose one from the list below). The organizer should make it more likely that children will notice or explain the relationship.

Some topics to choose from (or develop an organizer for one of your own topics):

- The things that plants need to grow.
- Squashing, bending, twisting and stretching.
- Choosing the right material for the job.
- Cool in summer – warm in winter.
- Solids, liquids and gases.
- Natural and manufactured materials.

What is the understanding that this organizer could support? How might you use it?

Graphic organizers in practical work

Another kind of graphic organizer has been used to help children grasp the possibilities in a situation, such as in an investigation. For instance, suppose the topic is about *Light and shadows*. If one of the activities for the children was to make 'shadow' pictures using coloured sugar paper, different objects could be laid on a sheet of paper and left in the sunlight for a day or two. The colour of the paper fades except under the object and so leaves a 'shadow'. You ask the children what makes good shadows and present the possibilities in a concise way as a picture (Figure 3.6). You should, of course, expect reasons for their ideas. The picture is, in effect, an extension of each child's mental notepad and acts as an aide-mémoire.

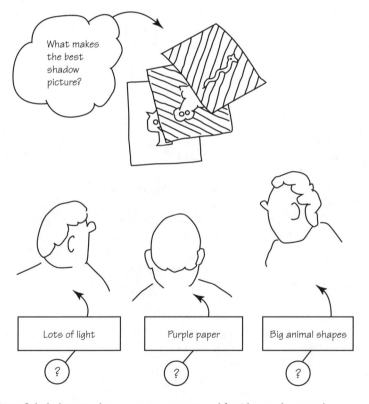

Figure 3.6 A diagram that serves as a memo pad for ideas to be tested

Graphic organizers can summarize quite complex procedures and make them manageable for young children. This makes them very useful in practical work. There is a danger, however, that they substitute for understanding. For this reason, it is more useful to construct such an organizer with the involvement of the children. They might, for instance, predict each step of a procedure and explain why it is appropriate. Later, the graphic organizer can be used to check understanding by adding 'Why?' boxes to each step. The children have to tell you in their own words the purpose of those steps. Another version is to list a relatively long procedure and cut it into its individual steps. The children have to put it in order and justify the sequence.

Not all organizers to do with practical work will show the steps of a procedure. For example, some can support children's thinking by providing them with a way of recording information. One might be a set of circles for sorting and recording results. Another could be columns for listing objects with and without certain features. Simple keys for identifying plants and animals can also be graphic organizers because they structure and sequence a child's thought.

Activity pictures

You are about to have the children do a practical activity. Try designing graphic organizers that will:

- help them see the possibilities that the activity could offer
- help them understand the procedure involved
- help them record results in a way that makes it more likely that the children will notice a relevant pattern.

Some topics to choose from (or develop organizers for those you will have to teach):

- Not all flowers are the same.
- How fast does grass grow?
- Taking the sand out of some sandy water by filtering.
- What is it that makes a good oven glove?
- What is it that makes some stones 'skip' over water?

Analogies presented graphically

Analogies can be powerful aids to understanding and they do not have to be complicated to help a child grasp some relationship. For example, an orange can serve as an analogy for the earth. To us, living on the earth's surface, there are enormous hills and deep valleys. To a tiny bug on an orange, it seems just the same. We can get a feel for the bug's point of view if we look at an orange skin with a hand lens. The bug would have to struggle up the orange's hills and run down into its valleys. But, from a distance, the orange looks smooth. It is just the same with the earth: from a distance, we cannot see its hills and valleys so it looks like a smooth ball.

If what you use in the analogy is familiar to the children (as an orange is likely to be), it stands a good chance of supporting their understanding. Some analogies are common in science and teachers plan to use them beforehand. Often, however, you make an analogy on the spot in response to a lack of comprehension. A quick sketch on the board can be a powerful aid that highlights the parallels you want to draw. In the case of the orange and earth, for instance, you might draw lines to connect similar features as you make your point (Figure 3.7).

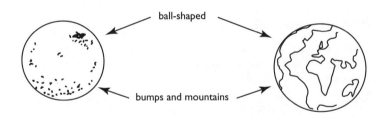

Figure 3.7 An analogy between an orange and the earth

Figure 3.8 shows an analogy that relates life in the sea to life on land. The intention is to make connections between the two environments. Since the children are familiar with one (life on the land), they can use it to understand life in the other. In other words, life on the land serves as an analogy for a grasp of parallel niches in the sea.

Analogies support understanding by relating what is to be understood to something that is already well understood. They do, however, have to be used with care. First, children need to be familiar with what you will use as the basis of your analogy (the orange or life on the land in these examples). Second, analogies can be taken too far. For instance, we do

Figure 3.8 A graphic organizer depicting life on the land and in the air as an analogy for life in the sea

not want the children to think that the earth contains pips or has a stalk pit like an orange. Similarly, we would not want children to believe that fish behave like birds in every respect. The risk of this can be reduced by looking for some differences: 'Is an orange *exactly* like the earth?' 'Do fish behave *exactly* like birds?' could be talk you might use to start things off for these analogies.

Pictorial analogies

Is there a simple analogy you might draw to help the children understand a topic you will teach in science (or choose one from the list below)?

- the strength of leg bones
- solids, liquids and gases
- sound travelling through air

- Sketch a picture you could use to construct a graphic organizer during focused talk with the children. (The picture will probably have two parts, connected by lines, as in the example shown earlier.)
- How might you ensure that the children are familiar with the basis of the analogy?
- How might you make the analogy (that is, draw attention to the parallels)?
- How might you reduce the risk that the children will take the analogy too far or too literally?

3.9 CUMULATIVE SUMMARY

This part has been about how to work with teaching and learning aids so that you maximize the effectiveness of both the aid and the talk. If you use an artefact, a picture or a story, for instance, the lesson is still in your control. These things can enrich and add meaning to the talk. If you use a videotape, computer software or follow a textbook, your lesson may be in the hands of the writers. This is not a loss when they enhance the quality of learning. You can increase the likelihood that this will be so by preparing the children for them, supporting them while they are in use and following through afterwards. In short, the aim is to make a good fit between these resources and the children's needs.

Earlier, what focused talk can do for understanding in science was described and illustrated. Here, ways of making it more effective and how

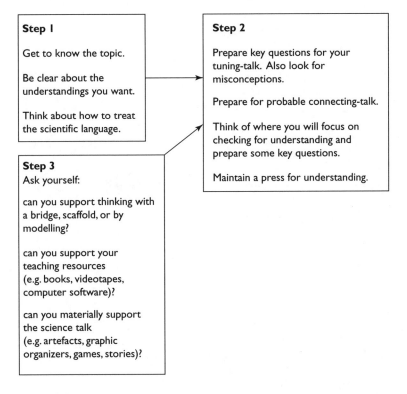

Figure 3.9 Summary chart

to use it to make the most of your teaching resources have been added. At this stage, you will often be in control of the talk, steering it towards your targets. This kind of dialogue is valuable because it can help to establish understandings. These understandings can still be somewhat vague, inconsistent and uncertain. The children need opportunities to reveal faults, iron out uncertainties and practise expressing and reformulating their thoughts. In the process, they make their grasp of their new learning more sure. This is addressed in the next part.

Figure 3.9 shows three steps for planning talk in science.

Part 4

Conversations in science

The strategies described so far should help children develop understandings but, at this early stage, these understandings may neither hang together well nor be well integrated with existing knowledge. As a result, they may be relatively fragile, impermanent and hard to use. This part describes ways of making them more secure and more useful. So far, you will usually have been in control of the science talk, directing attention, giving thinking a fairly narrow focus and checking that mental connections are being made. The children probably expect that to be the case and wait for you to take the lead. Although you will encourage them to respond at length, you have clear targets and aim to achieve them in that lesson. Consequently, digressions are relatively limited and attention is directed to the immediate task in hand. Children, for a variety of reasons, play the game and ignore any niggling inconsistencies they feel. This can produce an understanding that is more or less detached and limited in value and durability. There needs to be some opportunities for children to reveal gaps and inconsistencies and make them good. To mark this change in emphasis, the word *conversation* has been used. Again, *T* indicates teacher talk and *C* indicates children's talk.

4.1 CONVERSATIONS IN SCIENCE

Through tuning and connecting-talk, we generally establish at least a germ of an understanding. This is just a beginning. The concepts and relationships may still be strange to the children. In their minds, there may be contradictions and areas of fuzzy confusion. Conventions and ideas that we use with ease can seem strange and obscure to them. At this stage, there will be aspects of the topic that have not been grasped at all, that have been grasped in part, that appear to have been grasped well but have not, and that have been grasped well but are not integrated with other areas of knowledge as well as they might be. After all, a lesson or two does not provide much time to explore ideas, become familiar with them, relate them to others, try them out and, in short, make them their own. Contrast that with the effect of everyday experience. Just because it is every day we tend to learn from it (although not always in an uncommon sense way). The children's somewhat delicate under-standings need cultivation.

Our aim is for children to establish a meaningful and a well-integrated understanding of the topic. Science conversations are intended to support that process. They provide opportunities for children to reveal and talk through their understandings and organize, extend and apply them more widely. How is a science conversation different from tuning, connecting and monitoring-talk in science? A loose parallel is in the difference between a conversation between friends and an interview for a job. In an interview, to some extent you try to say what you believe the interviewers want to hear and you look for clues that point you to that. The interviewers are in control and are judging every word. Contrast that with how you behave in a conversation. You often risk revealing more about your thoughts than you would in an interview. In a conversation, less hangs on a particular response and you are more likely to say what you really think and reveal what you cannot do. You feel able to introduce an idea of your own and explore it. You can ask what others think and include that in your own idea. And you probably enjoy a conversation more than an interview. A conversation in science is intended to have some of these characteristics. In particular, it should:

- be in a non-judgemental context in order to encourage children to express their understandings fully, warts and all
- be interesting so that the children will want to talk science in a conversation
- provide opportunities for all to participate

- be flexible so that it can go in unexpected directions, and
- be unhurried in order to allow time for thought and talk.

A non-judgemental context is intended to encourage children to express their understandings openly. If they know that they can say something that turns out to be 'wrong' and not be marked down for it, they are more likely to talk about what they believe to be the case rather than what they think you believe to be the case. A formal setting, with the teacher standing over and dominating the class, firing a barrage of questions at them, is unlikely to give the children this kind of security. You may prefer a less formal arrangement in which the children and you sit as a group.

Children are more likely to engage in protracted science conversations if they perceive the topic to be relevant to their needs and interests. They are generally interested in things to do with themselves, their place in the world, the adults they will become, and in their growing competence. For instance, children like to get the measure of things so the very large and the very small attract their attention (perhaps a part of knowing the world and their place in it). They will often rise to a challenge so setting a problem may draw them in (probably because it relates to their feelings of competence). A story they can relate to may also stimulate interest (interest in themselves and who they might become). Some things interest children the world over. For instance, a question from a small boy in San Francisco, sent to *New Scientist*, asks how long it will take for his recently deceased guinea pig to 'become just bones' (14 October 2000). It is likely that this curiosity about life, death and change, with a dash of morbid interest, is not confined to one culture and location. But other interests may be culture and even situation specific. What seems relevant to one group of children may not be so to another. Topics of real interest, however, motivate children to talk because they satisfy some psychological need. Feeling cannot be divorced from thinking.

Whether or not a topic will catch the children's interest can also depend on how you present it but any conversation is likely to be short if a teacher's monotone indicates little interest in the children or the topic. If you are inclined to be enthusiastic, all the better. Your enthusiasm can draw children into an activity and increase the attention they give it. It indicates to the children that you find the conversation interesting and worthwhile. If you are not someone who is naturally enthusiastic, it is worth showing your interest. Even feigned enthusiasm has been found to be effective with children.

Some children may dominate a conversation while others sit quietly. Interaction in a large group may be intimidating for some and could inhibit their participation. If you find this to be the case, you may try working with smaller groups to develop the confidence of those who are timid. At the same time, some children have learned that if they sit quietly they are left to themselves. Working with smaller groups provides a greater opportunity to include them in the conversation.

Conversations can take an unexpected turn. While experience will teach you where they tend to go, they could go anywhere. A child may have read, seen or heard something that he or she believes to be relevant and so talks about it. The contribution should not be dismissed; it is, after all, a conversation with the children, not an interrogation. If it really is irrelevant, it is better if the child comes to that conclusion for him or herself. Care is needed, however, as what might seem to be irrelevant at first is relevant when the child's thinking becomes clear. There will be occasions when you are asked a question that you cannot answer. This should not be a cause for concern. After all, it can happen in any conversation. You may reflect the question to the group for them to talk about or, if the question lends itself to practical work, you may take the opportunity to explore it that way.

This can take time: time to form thoughts, time to express them, time to listen and think about them, and time to help the child explore ideas. Conversations need to be unhurried. They are probably easier to initiate and maintain if the children have at least a little background knowledge. On this basis, the natural place for conversations is after you have developed the background. But this does not mean that it is the only place for a conversation. Children are not empty-headed and often bring knowledge with them. Where there is prior knowledge, a conversation may help to sort it out, relate parts together and prepare the way for further learning. In other words, while you may feel conversations are a way of rounding off a topic, in some topics, they may be a way of starting it.

Whenever you decide to use a conversation, planning is important. There may be occasions when off-the-cuff conversations are brilliantly successful but, in general, you will want to plan how you will arrange the class, initiate the conversation and maintain it. This is not to say that you will have planned every question and observation and every direction a conversation will take. It simply means that you know how you will start and maintain it.

How to make opportunities for conversations in science will now be described. Remember that, in a conversation, the emphasis is on fostering extended discussions that let the children reveal, mend, adjust, extend and use their understandings. Do remember that the instruments that provide the opportunities are no more than instruments. So, for instance, a picture, story or poem can be an instrument for stimulating a conversation. They could, of course, also be used to provide specific support for tuning-talk or connecting-talk, as was illustrated earlier. But instruments like these are not tied to a particular kind of support: what you get out of them depends on how you use them.

4.2 CONVERSATIONS FROM EVENTS

Probably the most natural conversations we have stem from events: things that happen to us, what we read about, what we hear, and what we see. With children, we can take opportunities as they occur. They may, for instance, be about:

- extremes of weather (gales, snow storms, floods, droughts, fog, lightning)
- other natural phenomena that occur anywhere in the world (comets, eclipses, volcanic eruptions, earthquakes, landslides, meteor showers)
- technological novelty (space station, electric cars, new toys)
- local happenings (building, digging, draining, planting, repairing).

What makes these potentially interesting for children is that they are new to them and, in some cases, they can be at an extreme. What makes them useful depends on how you relate them to the science you have been doing. Events, by their nature, do not happen at a time that suits you so you may find it helps if you keep news cuttings, tapes of news items and, at times, engineer events so that they happen when and where you want them. For example, as you approach the end of a topic on packaging materials, you allow a variety of litter to accumulate so you can complain about the mess. This gives you an opportunity to begin a conversation about litter and its effect on the quality of life and the durability of some packaging materials compared with those that are biodegradable.

Another kind of event is the visit. You take the children to the seashore or the farm and, in addition to the formal work you had planned, what they see there can provide the basis of a conversation. For instance, 'Have you noticed how pebbles on the beach are usually smooth? I wonder why that is?' might stimulate some extended speculation and exploration. A visitor to the school could also provide the context for science talk. For example, after a visit by a nurse, there could be conversations relating to *Ourselves* or *Germs* and what to do about them.

Eventful times

Here are some brief examples of using events to initiate conversations. 'A lack of friction' is an illustration with younger children; 'Powerless' is an illustration with older children.

A lack of friction

Some of the children slipped on the icy slide made by the older ones. The teacher saw it happen and directed them to a different route. In the classroom, she gained everyone's attention.

'Listen, everyone. I saw some of you slip on the ice. Sanjeev, can you tell everyone what happened?'

Sanjeev does so and the teacher, adopting a relaxed pose, says,

'You know, I've seen this happen before. I wonder where the ice came from.'

The children respond and the teacher asks what makes ice so slippery. They discuss the dangers of ice on pavements and make suggestions about how ice could be made less dangerous. They discuss the alternatives and decide which would be the best way of making ice less slippery.

Powerless

One dark day in winter, there is a power cut and the classroom is plunged into gloom for about ten minutes. The children cannot see well enough to read or write so the teacher takes the opportunity to have a conversation.

'Do you think it's just our school that has no electricity? I wonder if it's off everywhere. What if the traffic lights are off?'

This begins speculation about all the things we take for granted that use electricity and what life would be like without it. It establishes the enormous dependency we have on sources of energy like electricity. The conversation could continue with thoughts about what people did before they had electricity in the home.

Seizing the moment

Choose one of the following events and consider how it might be used to initiate a conversation in science:

- There are roadworks near the school. A very large hole has been dug showing a cross-section of soil and subsoil.
- The people who remove the refuse did not come today and the children have been warned to keep away from the storage containers.

- The drains on the road have become blocked and the street is flooded because the heavy rain had nowhere to go.
- The Parent-Teachers Association held a flower show in the school hall. Afterwards, some of the flowers have been used to decorate the classrooms.
- Once again, the trains have been delayed because of 'leaves on the lines'.
- A hot air balloon flies over the school.

4.3 CONVERSATIONS FROM CHILDREN'S QUESTIONS

Ideas for conversations may also, of course, come from the children. The children may ask questions or make an observation that you could use as a starting point. For instance, suppose a child showed you a small cut on her hand. You would be inclined to direct her to the wash basin with instructions to wash it clean. But, when she returned, you could also use it to start a conversation about cuts, germs, blood and the need for hygiene and antiseptics. Suppose a child asked about what it was like when the dinosaurs were alive. You might direct him to the book shelf to read about it. But, after a while, you could start a conversation with what he had found out. During work on sound, a child mentions that she has seen people wear 'plastic ear muffs'. You could tell her that they are called 'ear defenders' and they stop loud noise from damaging your ears. Or, you could offer it to the class and develop a conversation about what loud noises might do to ears, how ear defenders work and what might be used instead in an emergency.

If the children generally do not ask questions spontaneously, you could try a Questions Box. This is rather like a suggestion box but is for 'things you would really like to know about this topic'. The children write their inquiries in the form of a letter and post them to you. (This is an occasion when working singly could be better than group work as real concerns may be lost in a child's desire to conform.) When you read the questions, you may find that they can be sorted into coherent clusters, each cluster giving you a conversation topic.

Another kind of conversation that can exercise the children's grasp of science is the '*I wonder what it would be like if you . . .*' game. For instance, if you have been examining a log of wood, counting the rings to find its age, looking at how the rings vary in thickness and discussing how differences in the weather can cause such variations, you might finish by saying, 'I wonder what it would be like if you had been that tree'. The children then talk about the tree's life from its beginning to its end. Some other examples are:

- I wonder what it would be like if you were a bee (talking about, for instance, the bee's role in pollination).
- I wonder what it would be like if you were a wheat seed (talking about the seed's germination, growth, harvesting and making into bread).
- I wonder what it would be like if you were a caterpillar (talking

about the life cycle of the butterfly; see also Eric Carle's story, *The Very Hungry Caterpillar*, published by Hamish Hamilton Childrens Books, London, 1994).

- I wonder what it would be like if you were a raindrop (talking about the rain cycle).
- I wonder what it would be like if you were a ray of light (talking about its arrow-like flight and regular reflection from smooth, flat surfaces).
- I wonder what it would be like if you were a magnet (talking about, for instance, what it does as it is carried around in someone's pocket).
- I wonder what it would be like if you were an Incredibly Tiny Person (talking about, for example, being small enough to be comparable with the size of a germ).

However, care is needed with this game. Children must not lose sight of reality. The tree does not 'see' all those years of history or 'feel' the erosion around its roots in the way we see and feel. Similarly, we may give the bee and the caterpillar feelings and motives they may not possess and, of course, a magnet is not aware of its surroundings at all. As this is a science lesson, it can be a real concern but it is not insurmountable. Where there is a danger that the children will believe such liberties, we could add, for example, 'If only bees really were like people. How much like people do you think they really are?'

Engaging conversations

If your interest is in teaching younger children:

I wonder

What topic in science might these conversation starters relate to? How would you handle the conversations?

- 'I wonder what it would be like if you were a grasshopper.'
- 'I wonder what it would be like if you were a raindrop.'
- 'I wonder what it would be like if you were a toy car at the top of a big, steep hill and the handbrake broke.'

If your interest is in teaching older children:

Some electrifying questions

This is a cluster of questions about electricity. How would you use them in a conversation?

- Why doesn't electricity run out of batteries when you turn them upside down?
- What's in a battery?
- Why do batteries have 'volts' on them?

4.4 CONVERSATIONS FROM ARTEFACTS

Artefacts are natural conversation pieces. There must be many occasions when you had a conversation that started with 'Have you seen this?' An artefact can catch interest and provide a concrete focus for expressing understandings. Of course, you may have to initiate and help to maintain the conversation. Having something ready to say can help. For instance, you might say:

- Look what I've just found!
- Do you know what happened to me this morning?
- What on earth is it?
- It reminds me of something. I wonder what it is?
- I wonder what it's made from.
- What does it do?
- Do you think it still works? Let's try it out.
- Who might use it?
- How would you use it?
- I've always wondered about that! Isn't that interesting?

At the same time, try to make the most of the unexpected. Suppose, for instance, a child brings in a fossil. You could ask her what it is and praise her for her interest. But you could also show interest yourself: 'Oh, that's interesting. I wonder what it looked like when it was alive? What do you think?' As this interested a child enough to make the effort to bring it to you, it is likely that it will interest others in the class, too.

Do remember, however, that these are devices for stimulating a science conversation and not a question and answer session. You do not want children to answer briefly then wait in silence for your next question.

Matters of artefact

Here are some examples. 'A skull' is in a lesson for younger children, 'Keeping cool' is with older children.

A skull

Earlier, the class has been learning about the internal framework of the human body, that is, its skeleton. They had seen X-ray pictures showing broken bones, the skull and the rib cage. They had felt some bones in their own bodies and made model skeletons from card tubes and boxes, using string for joints. To conclude, the teacher decided to try a science conversation and produced an animal's skull from the cupboard.

'Look what I've found in the cupboard. What is it?'

'It's a skull!' announced the children, coming closer. They made various observations about its teeth, their size and shape, the places where the eyes would be and the way the lower jaw articulated.

'I wonder what it was?' mused the teacher, looking it full in the face. Various suggestions came in rapid succession from the children. The teacher talked through each possibility with the children, considering the evidence. Based on the length of the jaw and the teeth, they decided that it was probably a dog's skull. The teacher continued to show interest in the skull.

'Isn't it like people's skulls? I mean, do you remember the X-ray picture? Look, there it is, on the window. It's amazing, isn't it?' The children agreed. 'I wonder how many things are the same. I'll bet there are lots.' The children begin to name them. When they had exhausted the possibilities, the teacher counted the similarities and announced the figure, showing some astonishment. The children responded similarly. 'I wonder how many differences there are', he said, and the children identified differences and he listed them. At the end, they were all surprised that there were more things the same in their list than there were things that were different. The conversation took a slightly different direction at this point when someone mentioned dinosaur bones.

The children's interest in the skull facilitated the conversation. The teacher himself showed interest, curiosity and astonishment but he did not parade his own knowledge and did not let it dominate the talk. If a question went unanswered, he did not force it but was inclined to let the conversation take its own course to some extent. He was, however, careful to give it a new direction when it flagged. In the process, the conversation let him see what, as a group, the children understood. It also widened their understanding. In this instance, the activity was for the whole class but it could have taken place with a smaller group and even with one child.

Keeping warm

A previous lesson was about keeping warm when climbing in the Himalayas. The children had tested a variety of materials and found which was the best for retaining heat. They put the materials in order of effectiveness and examined their structure, relating it to each material's ability to retain heat. The teacher shows them how aluminium foil is used to wrap up people suffering from exposure to the cold. They try it and agree that it keeps the heat in. The teacher decides to develop a conversation.

'My house used to be really cold. Every winter we were freezing. Do you know what we did about it?' There was little response so the teacher showed them a large piece of loft insulation (sealed in a transparent bag). 'We put this in the loft . . . rolls of it, all over. It covers the whole of the loft floor.' The children looked at it and squashed the bag.

'We've got that in our loft, Miss', said one girl.

'Oh? Is yours the same?'

'Nearly. It's just a different colour.'

'It's supposed to be good stuff', said the teacher. 'It was very expensive so I hope it works. I wonder how it works.'

The children were keen to give her the benefit of their knowledge and explained that it was like wool and had lots of air in it so it kept the heat in. One added that it was called lagging and it could be put around water tanks 'to keep them warm'.

'So how's that work?' she asked. Explanations came from several children. When they subsided, the teacher took out a length of draught-excluding tape and said she had also fitted this around the doors and windows. The children were keen to tell her why and that she should leave places for fresh air to get in. They talk about why that is important.

'Oh, that's good. We did that. Look at what else we did. We've put on some special wallpaper. Here's a piece', she said. The children commented on how nice it looks but the teacher directed their attention to the feel and thickness of the wallpaper.

'It feels warm', observed one. The others felt it and agree.

'Yes, I thought that, too', agreed the teacher. 'Isn't it strange?'

'Why's it feel warm, Miss?' asked one boy. The teacher did not respond but allowed others to answer:

'It just feels it, it's not really warm!'

'It's the heat from your hand. It can't go anywhere so it, sort of, comes back at you.'

'Polystyrene feels like that.'

The children were really curious about this effect and held the material next to their cheeks, confirming that it feels warm. It became clear that some thought the material was producing heat itself. Even those who thought otherwise were uncertain about why the material should feel warm. While they accepted that heat can be reflected from a surface, they did not seem to see themselves as a source of heat of any significance. The teacher reminded them of what it was like in the classroom with only one or two people in it compared with when the classroom is full. The children were intrigued by the thought that each of them is a mini-heater and they speculated wildly about how many people it would take to be boiled alive in the classroom.

The teacher allowed the children a brief glimpse into her private world. She took care not to display her knowledge but let them explain things to her. In the process, they became intrigued by the action of the special wallpaper and this revealed inconsistencies and gaps in their understandings. In thinking of themselves as heaters, the conversation also allowed the children a chance to play with their understandings. Being able to play like this suggests that they have a fair grasp of the idea.

Artefacts as conversation pieces

Choose one or two of the following artefacts and think about how you would use them to provide opportunities for children to talk about their science.

- a freshly cut log
- a fruit
- a spider
- a hard hat

Think about how you would manage the conversation so that it

- engaged the children's interest
- provided opportunities for relatively long verbal responses from the children
- provided opportunities for them to explore what the ideas mean to them
- provided opportunities for them to share and evaluate their ideas.

4.5 CONVERSATIONS FROM PICTURES

Like artefacts, pictures can also stimulate a science conversation. There are times when you are not able to show some science or it may not be safe or possible to take children to see the science for themselves. When this is the case, a picture may have to suffice. It can be a very good substitute, as when a picture reminds the children of something that is already familiar to them. For instance, after finding out what happens to pools of water on warm, windy days and comparing it with what happens on cool, still days, the children might be shown a picture of a line of washing blowing in the breeze. The aim would be to stimulate a conversation that relates the scene to the understanding of evaporation under different conditions.

Sometimes, the picture puts events in an interesting and meaningful context for the children. A picture of Winnie the Pooh hauling friends into a tree house with a rope and pulley may not be strictly realistic but it can still be useful. For instance, it could be used with young children who have been classifying forces. Single pulleys used for changing the direction of a pull are not such common sights today as they once were and many young children may never have seen one in use. The conversation could aim to explore the function of this strange item.

On other occasions, the picture may show a phenomenon the children have not seen before. Here, you will need to ensure that the children grasp what the picture shows. For instance, after observing the way hot air rises above radiators, you might show the children a picture of hot air balloons floating high over some fields. You would need to explore it carefully with the children, making sure they have noticed that each balloon has a device hanging under it for heating the air. The aim is to prepare them for a conversation that includes explanations of hot-air balloon action.

Here are some examples of pictures used to stimulate a science conversation. 'Hear all' relates to work with younger children; 'Hearing aids' is with older children.

Just picture it

Hear all

Following work on sound, the teacher asks the children what they think their ear flaps are for. They say that they are to hear with. He shows them a picture of a bird.

'Can a bird hear?' he asks. The children think they can but obviously feel uncomfortable about the contradiction.

'Yes, I think that birds can hear, just like us', the teacher confides. 'When they are in my garden, all I have to do is clap my hands and they fly away. But birds don't have ear flaps like us so I wonder what our ear flaps are for?'

Some inconclusive conversation follows after which he shows them a picture of a cat that is obviously attending to some noise. The children speculate on the purpose of its movable ears. One child suggests that they are to 'look' at noises. The teacher shows interest and encourages her to elaborate. She explains that the cat in the picture is listening to something. The teacher agrees and asks himself (aloud) where the noise might be coming from. A number of children indicate the appropriate direction.

'I wonder what it would be like to have ears like that? What do you think?' asks the teacher. The children speculate, some putting their hands behind their ears to make them bigger.

'That's a good idea. Let's try it! Let's make some big ears and see what they do.' The children make ears from card and try them out, noting that they can improve hearing in a particular direction. The teacher returns to the picture of the bird. 'I wonder what it's like being a bird. They have no flappy bits. I'm not going to cut off my ears to see what it's like. I think we can guess what it's like to hear without our flappy bits.'

The children talk about the advantages and disadvantages of having ear flaps and movable ears. The teacher shows them a picture of a vulture, a bird without feathers on its head, and points out the entrance to the ear (Figure 4.1). The children see this as confirmation that birds lack ear flaps.

In what could be the beginning of an extended conversation, the teacher used a mix of pictures of animals and real objects (ears and card extensions to ears). Some questions appeared to be directed to himself.

Figure 4.1 The first birds had no apparent ears while those of the cat are obvious; without feathers, the way into the bird's (vulture's) ear is visible

The outcome was a clarification of the function of the parts of the ear and a greater understanding of animals' hearing.

Hearing aids

Following work in sound, the teacher pretends to mishear someone and has to ask him to repeat what he said.

'Maybe I need a hearing aid!' she says. 'Do you know what hearing aids look like?' The children say they do and try to describe one.

'I'll help you. I've got a picture of one', and the teacher produces a picture of a hearing trumpet from the nineteenth century. The children stare at it for a second.

'Miss, it's the wrong picture! That's not a hearing aid!'

The teacher looks at it as though to check and then says that it really is a hearing aid. After a brief pause, she adds,

'. . . from Victorian times. Do you remember when we were doing the Victorians in history?' The children stare more closely. One asks,

'How does it work? Does it have batteries?'

The teacher quickly makes a paper cone and shows the children how to use it as a hearing trumpet (Figure 4.2). The children want to know if it works so she gives them some paper and they try it. They talk about how it catches more sound.

'Here's another picture. Come and have a look. This is how to talk to someone in another room without using a telephone.' This picture showed a Victorian speaking tube. 'It's a bit of a puzzle, this one. I wonder how it works. Look at the way the tube bends all over.'

The children stare at the picture for a few seconds and offer explanations. They talk of sound going around the tube until it leaves the other end. The teacher listens to all suggestions and asks them to point

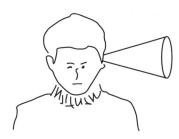

Figure 4.2 A simple hearing trumpet made from thin card

out the path that the sound takes. Some children draw curved lines through the tube; others are inclined towards straight lines and depict reflections from the inner walls of the tube.

'Hmm! I wonder who's right', ponders the teacher and the children try to justify their own explanations to one another. One reminds the others of the time they made echoes by banging together two dustbin lids out on the school field. Afterwards, they had drawn sound going straight to the school wall and bouncing off again. Following this, they were silent for a few seconds and began to come to a consensus about the likely path taken by the sound.

In this instance, the teacher did not have a Victorian ear trumpet to show the children so a picture was used instead. In effect, it made the conversation possible.

Talking pictures

Choose one of the pictures described below and think about how you would use it to initiate science talk. In particular, think about how you would manage the talk so that

- it provides opportunities for relatively long responses from the children
- it provides opportunities for them to explore what things mean to them
- it provides opportunities for them to share and evaluate their ideas.

Picture 1: a group of placid looking dinosaurs eating foliage while a different kind of dinosaur creeps up on them.
Picture 2: a moonscape, taken on the moon's surface and showing the earth rising in the background.

4.6 CONVERSATIONS FROM STORIES AND POEMS

Stories and poems often describe an event and you may use them as a substitute for the event itself. Stories and poems, however, provide their information through words. Each child has to interpret the words and build a mental picture of what is going on. This can contribute to and practise children's literacy skills and, at the same time, stimulate a conversation in science. In turn, this conversation practises a child's communication skills. Altogether, this can make using stories and poems in science an efficient use of time.

Stories and poems can tell a tale. Plots unfold, events occur and problems develop. Children often find them interesting and worth talking about. All you need is some good material that relates to the understandings you want to develop. That is not always as easy as it may sound. Some traditional tales and poems predate the time when science and technology had a major impact on thought and life and do not relate easily to what you have to teach. Nevertheless, there are stories that could be used to support teaching in subjects such as science (see also Further Reading).

Humanizing science

Traditionally, science is reported without reference to the people who did it but this does not mean it must be taught like that. Sometimes, putting people back into the science can have advantages:

- It can show scientists as real people, much like people the children might know (and unlike the 'mad scientist' common in some people's conceptions).
- It can provide a way of teaching something of the nature of science and the way people react to developments in it (as in, for instance, illustrating that just because you do an experiment that supports your theory, it does not mean that everyone will immediately accept it).
- It can show science as being relevant to people's needs (as illustrated by 'No Lollipop Today' (pp. 140–1), in which the properties of materials make a difference to the crossing patrol person's work).

Here are some examples of stories and poems that could be used to stimulate a science conversation.

Conversations from stories and poems

Following a topic such as *Keeping warm*, 'Ollie's Coat' could be used to stimulate a conversation about the heat retaining properties of various materials and how wild animals cope with the seasons by 'changing their coats'.

Ollie's Coat

Ollie was an owl, proud of his coat,
Two-tone brown, thick with down;
Whatever the weather, never lost a feather,
Until one day, he went to play,
And his feathers blew away!

'Whooo!' said Ollie, proud of his coat,
'Feathers in a sack! Take them back!
Here, Mum, quick! Stick! Stick! Stick!'
'Now, then, son; nothing's to be done.
Your coat's all gone!'

'Ooooh!' said Ollie, proud of his coat,
Two-tone brown, thick with down,
One minute there, next minute bare.
But wait and see! Coats are free,
For owls like Ollie.

The poem describes Ollie's first moult. It might be used to support the understanding that animals' coats (fur and feather) are not permanent and may change to suit the season. Some talk to help things along could be:

- Oh, dear! What's happened to Ollie?
- Do birds lose their feathers? Have you ever found a feather?
- Look at these feathers that I found. Why do birds have feathers?
- Which feathers do you think would keep Ollie warm in winter? Why?
- What will Ollie's new coat be like when he's ready for the winter?
- To widen the conversation a little: Why do ducks have 'down'? Why does an eiderdown keep us warm? What about dogs and cats, do they have feathers? What happens to their fur? Animals that change colour in winter add another dimension to the conversation.

The dog who would not stop barking

This story is, in essence, about fair tests. What is it that makes Ben bark? How do we isolate and eliminate various things that might start his barking? This gives the story some potential for a conversation about what makes a scientific investigation. The context also provides a starting point for talking about the loudness of sound, noise and sound insulation. It could be used after the children have tried an investigation and might help them reflect upon it.

Ben is a quiet dog. All he wants to do is eat and sleep. Ben's owner, Simon, likes to spend his spare time doing odd jobs around the house. Usually, these odd jobs seem to make a lot of noise. Today was an odd job day and Ben could not find a peaceful place anywhere. Sharon, Simon's wife, didn't like the noise either but, today, she did not seem to mind. Humming to herself, she sorted out the papers to do with the van.

'Mmm', she muttered, 'better have it serviced soon.'

'Sharon', said Simon, putting down the hammer. There was no answer. 'Sharon!' he said, loudly. Still no answer. He went to find her. She was putting the papers into an envelope. 'Sharon'. There was still no answer. She did not even look at him. He touched her arm and she jumped with fright.

'Sorry', she said, taking out some small earplugs, 'but you make so much noise that I just had to do something'.

'Oh', he said, looking a little hurt. 'I need some nails so I'm going to the shop.'

'OK. I'll come with you. We'll call at the garage and book the van in for a service.'

Ben liked a quiet life but he wouldn't say no to a trip to the shops. There were boney things just at nose height and they smelled delicious. If he hung around them long enough, someone might buy him one. Anyway, it was worth a try. But this is where I should tell you something else about Ben. He is a quiet dog but, if he does bark, it is loud and long. 'Woof! Woof! Woof! Woof! Woof! Woof! Woof! Woof! Woof! Woof! Woof!' he says, and 'Wooooof! he adds, without stopping for breath.

Sharon and Simon collected their things and headed for the door. So did Ben.

'Oh', said Sharon, seeing Ben.

'Oh-Oh', said Simon. Ben's tail wagged.

'Oh, come on then', said Sharon and Ben dashed to the back of the van.

'Here we go again', complained Simon. You see, Ben really is a quiet dog . . . but not in the van. At every other time, all he does is eat and sleep. It drives Sharon and Simon crazy. They feed him, take him for walks, bath him, cover him with flea powder, have him injected at the vet's, brush his fur and make his bed. They know Ben as well as they know each other but they can't figure out why he barks in the van. They cannot go anywhere without that awful racket. 'Woof! Woof! Woof! Woof! Woof! Woof! Woof! Woof! Woof! Woof!' he says, when they stop at the traffic lights. Passers-by stare and wonder if they should call the RSPCA. 'Woof! Woof! Woof! Woof! Woof! Woof! Woof! Woof! Woof! Woof!' he says, as they go down the High Street. People in police cars look and wonder if they should stop and arrest them. 'Woof! Woof! Woof! Woof! Woof! Woof! Woof! Woof! Woof! Woof!' he says, as they go over the bridge and the back doors swing open. Fishermen look up from the river and wonder if they should call the bailiff.

Today was no different. They had hardly started when so did Ben.

'Woof! Woof! Woof! Woof! Woof! Woof! Woof! Woof! Woof! Woof!' he said. 'Woof! Woof! Woof! Woof! Woof! Woof! Woof! Woof! Woof! Woof!' he added, for good measure. Today he seemed worse than ever.

'It's no use!' said Sharon, 'We've got to find out what's making him bark. We can't go around like this forever. Let's go home. We'll have to think this through.'

As they drove home, Simon said, 'Maybe it's being cooped up with the doors shut'.

'Woof! Woof! Woof! Woof! Woof! Woof! Woof! Woof! Woof! Woof!' said Ben.

'Maybe it's all the bumping around', suggested Sharon.

'Woof! Woof! Woof! Woof! Woof! Woof! Woof! Woof! Woof! Woof!' said Ben.

'Maybe it's the noise', said Simon, 'after all, the van is due for a service!'

'Woof! Woof! Woof! Woof! Woof! Woof! Woof! Woof! Woof! Woof!' said Ben.

'We'll just have to test them all, one by one', said Sharon. 'Let's do it now. I can't stand it any more.'

They pulled up, switched off the engine and opened the van doors. Ben sat in the van and stared at them in silence.

'Just look at him now', said Sharon and Ben wagged his tail.

'Maybe it's the van doors', said Simon, 'Maybe he doesn't like to be shut in.'

'Let's try it', said Sharon and she slammed the doors. Ben stared at them both through the window, looking puzzled. He did not make a sound.

'Can't be that', said Simon. 'Maybe it's when the van moves. Let's push it and see.'

Leaving the van doors open and with a lot of effort, they made the van bump along the road in silence. Ben watched them with interest and without a sound.

'It's no good!' gasped Simon. 'What else is there?'

'Maybe it's the noise of the engine', suggested Sharon. 'Keep the doors open while I switch on.' She switched on the engine. Ben jumped to his feet.

'Woof! Woof! Woof! Woof! Woof! Woof! Woof! Woof! Woof! Woof!' he went.

'That's it!' said Sharon. 'That's it! It's the noise! That's what does it!'

Just to be sure, she switched the engine off and Ben stopped barking. As soon as she switched on again, Ben began to bark again.

'Well, now we know what it is but what can we do about it. We can't get far with the engine switched off!' Simon complained.

'I've got just the thing!' said Sharon, and she ran into the house. When she came out, she went straight to Ben and fumbled with his ears.

'Now give it a try', she said.

Simon slid into the driver's seat and started the engine. Brmmm! Brmmm! went the engine. Ben stared at them in silence.

'That's good!' said Simon. 'What did you do? Just rub his ears?'

'More than that', she said, 'Look!' and she lifted one of Ben's ears.

'Earplugs!' said Simon. 'What a cure!'

'Right!' said Sharon. 'Now to the shops!'

'Oh, yes. I need some nails', said Simon.

'And some more earplugs!' added Sharon. 'I think I'm going to need them and I'm not using those again!'

Some talk to help a conversation along could be:

- What are earplugs? How do they work?
- Do you think they got it right? Why do you think that?
- I wonder if they could have done their test another way. What do you think?
- It's a bit like when we did that experiment, isn't it? I was trying to think what is the same about it. Help me out a bit, would you?
- I wonder if we could have made the experiment better?

Telling tales

This story is about being seen and how certain colours help us be seen.

* What science is involved in this story?
* How might you use the story to stimulate a science conversation?

No Lollipop Today

I know someone who has a lollipop every day, well, nearly every day. It's so big that people stop, even if they are in a car or on a bus. Do you know who it is? It's the Lollipop Man! One day, the Lollipop Man woke up and thought, 'It's still dark. I'll go back to sleep!' and so he did.

'Clunk!' went the letter box, as the postwoman put a letter through it.

'What's that?' said the Lollipop Man, sitting up in bed. 'Oh, no! Look at the time. I'm late.' He jumped out of bed, put on his waterproof boots and coat and rushed out of the house into a dull, damp morning. When he arrived at the school, there were lots of children waiting to cross the road.

'Ah! I'm in time.' he said with relief. 'No one's tried to cross the road yet.'

Straight away, he gathered everyone together and he stepped out into the road, holding up his hand. Zoom! The Lollipop Man jumped off the road. The car didn't even slow down!

'That was close', said the Lollipop Man rather nervously as he stepped out again. Grooom! He jumped back again as a bus roared past.

'What's matter with people, today!' said the Lollipop Man, very annoyed. He stepped out very firmly this time and held up his hand. Throooom! roared the lorry, missing him by the thickness of a hair.

'Hey!' shouted the Lollipop Man, shaking his fist at the back of the lorry.

'What's up?' asked the policeman, on his way home after the night shift.

'No one is stopping today. This is dangerous. I just can't get anyone safely across the road.'

'I'm not surprised', said the policeman. 'Just look at yourself. Where's your white coat and where's your lollipop?'

The Lollipop Man looked at himself with surprise. In his hurry, he had put on his black overcoat and had forgotten to pick up his lollipop!

'Borrow my yellow waistcoat.' said the policeman. 'They'll see you in that.'

The postwoman had finished her round by now and she stopped to see what was going on.

'Put these on, as well.' she said, giving the Lollipop Man her orange gloves. 'They'll help.'

The newspaper girl had finished her deliveries, too, so she stopped.

'I have pink armbands. You can borrow them if you want', she said.

The Lollipop Man put on the yellow waistcoat, he put on the orange gloves, and he put on the pink armbands. He could see the lights of a car and a bus and a lorry as he walked nervously into the middle of the road. He held up his arm with a pink armband on it. He put up his hand with an orange glove on it. He stretched out his chest to fill the yellow waistcoat. And he got ready to jump!

But he didn't have to jump. First, came the car, then came the bus, and then came the lorry and they all came gently to a stop, one after another.

'Phew!' said the Lollipop Man. 'Come on, everyone. It's safe to cross now.'

After everyone was in school, the Lollipop Man gave the yellow waistcoat, the orange gloves and the pink armbands back to the policeman, the postwoman, and the newspaper girl with lots of thanks.

'I'll never forget my white coat and lollipop again!' he said.

The Flow of Blood

Not all stories are fiction. Here is a short passage describing the life and work of William Harvey.

- What science is involved?
- How might you use it to stimulate a science conversation?

You must have fallen down and grazed yourself at some time. Where does the blood come from? What does it do inside your body? A doctor called William Harvey thought it out a long time ago. William lived from 1578 to 1657.

In those days, you could only go to school if you could pay for the lessons. William had eight brothers and sisters but, fortunately for him, his father was rich enough to be able to send him to school. After he finished school, William trained to be a doctor and became quite well known.

At that time, people thought that the heart was there to make blood. They knew that we have tubes everywhere in our bodies and that blood flows through them but what makes the blood move was a mystery.

William did experiments and found out that blood flows away from the heart in tubes called arteries. He also found that it flows back to the heart through tubes called veins. But what is it that made the blood move? William found that it is the heart. The heart behaves like a pump. It pumps the blood to all the parts of your body through the arteries. The blood returns to your heart through the veins to start its journey again.

At first, no one believed William's explanation. We now know that what he said is true. We also know that blood takes useful materials to all parts of your body to keep you alive and healthy.

4.7 WHO TAKES THE INITIATIVE?

You should not be surprised if the children generally expect you to lead the way in subject-centred talk. After all, you have probably made it quite clear that you have certain targets and there is no time for idle chit-chat, or even chat that is not immediately relevant. This part, however, has been about encouraging children to have a say and even take the initiative. When they do take the initiative, ask why-questions or want you to make a prediction (What will happen if . . .?), a lesson can take an unexpected turn and the teacher may be unprepared and uncertain. Nevertheless, thoughtful questions, explanations and observations should be encouraged. This helps the children learn that these count in science. How do you deal with the unexpected, particularly when you do not have a ready answer? Do you need a bluffer's guide to science?

First, not knowing the answer is no threat to your self-esteem. However much you know, children have a way of asking questions that poke into odd corners and leave you at a loss. Science is no different from history or any other subject in this respect. An historian probably knows a lot about certain periods of the past but very little about other times. Similarly, a scientist may be an expert in one branch of science but feel uncertain in another. Even if you know the answer you may not be able to translate it into a meaningful, concise version at short notice. Not being able to answer a question should not dent your confidence and it should not stop you from turning the question into a scientific conversation with the class.

Second, although children's questions are unpredictable, some questions tend to be asked again and again. Finding out more can be a joint enterprise with the children. 'What a good question! I don't think I know the answer! Let's see if we can find out', said with some enthusiasm, can be a motivating and fruitful strategy for the children and yourself. The task becomes more than a mere exercise where the teacher knows the answer but refuses to reveal it. It can include both information search skills and practical inquiry. The children have to make sense of what they find so it can be explained to you and others. As a result, your own subject knowledge and confidence will grow as you teach and you are ready when that question occurs again.

Here is an example to show how an unexpected question could be dealt with. Some important responses are in italics. The numbers in parentheses are referred to at the end.

A killer plant

In a lesson about plant structure and growth, David says that he saw a film where a plant trapped a man and its roots grew into his body. 'Could that really happen?' he asks, looking nervously at the class geranium.

T: 'Well, David,' responds the teacher, feeling discomforted and probably trying to recall what she had read in her *Bumper Book of Plant Life*, '*I've never seen or heard of it in real life. What does everyone think?*' [Pause.] 'Jane?' (1)

C: 'It was only a film. All sorts of things happen in films that aren't real.'

T: 'Yes, that's true. *Let's think about it. Look at these roots. Feel them. Are they hard? Are they sharp?*' [The children try them.] '*Do you think they could make holes in you?*' (2)

C: 'No . . . but, maybe plants in Africa could!'

T: '*Yes, that's always possible, I suppose. Have you seen any plants around here that could do that?*' (3)

C: 'No.'

T: '*I haven't seen any either. After we finish here, you could have a look at the plant books in the library and check it out. When you've done that, you can tell us about it. That's a really interesting thought, David.*' (4)

In (1), the teacher offered the problem to the class. In (2), the teacher was drawing on her own general knowledge of plants, acknowledging the limits of that in (3). In (4), the question was made a matter for investigation (by a search for relevant information in books). The child was expected to report back and was encouraged with the final comment.

Dealing with the unexpected

Here are some questions children could ask. Imagine that you are asked these in a lesson and think about how to provide a constructive response.

- C: 'Miss, why did the dinosaurs die out?
- C: 'Mr Brown, do you think there are aliens?'
- C: 'What makes a rainbow?'
- C: 'Why do some plants have thorns on them?'

4.8 CUMULATIVE SUMMARY

This part has been about how to encourage and foster a science conversation. Children need opportunities to express and use their understandings to help to improve them. Conversations are meant to encourage children to explore, play with and extend what they are just beginning to grasp. More formal talk may not provide these opportunities to the same extent because the child is often intent on giving you responses he or she thinks you want. Conversations may be stimulated in a variety of ways, such as by using an artefact, a picture, a story or poem, or simply something a child says. At times, children's questions can be unexpected. When treated as an opportunity for joint learning, all can develop in understanding. Figure 4.3 collects together the steps for helping children talk sense in science.

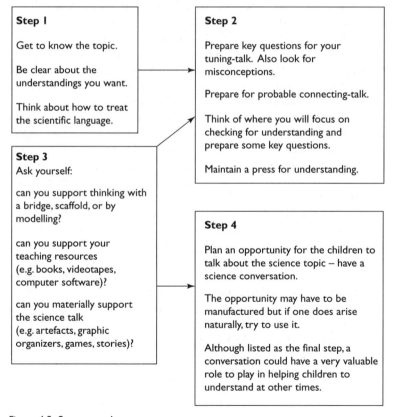

Step 1

Get to know the topic.

Be clear about the understandings you want.

Think about how to treat the scientific language.

Step 2

Prepare key questions for your tuning-talk. Also look for misconceptions.

Prepare for probable connecting-talk.

Think of where you will focus on checking for understanding and prepare some key questions.

Maintain a press for understanding.

Step 3
Ask yourself:

can you support thinking with a bridge, scaffold, or by modelling?

can you support your teaching resources (e.g. books, videotapes, computer software)?

can you materially support the science talk (e.g. artefacts, graphic organizers, games, stories)?

Step 4

Plan an opportunity for the children to talk about the science topic – have a science conversation.

The opportunity may have to be manufactured but if one does arise naturally, try to use it.

Although listed as the final step, a conversation could have a very valuable role to play in helping children to understand at other times.

Figure 4.3 Summary chart

Endnote

By the time you reach this point, I hope you will have seen the potential of oral interaction in science lessons and tried it for yourself. This does not mean that what you have done in the past is worthless. Purposeful, hands-on activity, testing ideas, going on field trips, reading books, finding information with ICT (information and communication technology) and much more remain legitimate and valuable ways of learning in science. However, asking and answering questions, discussing, debating, and talking together can make the most of the experience and enrich it with a wider, deeper and enduring understanding.

Certain kinds of talk matter more than others. What the children already know is very important because what you want them to understand must be tied to it. Talk which brings relevant prior knowledge into conscious thought makes it available for use and ready for connections. Talk which helps children process information, make connections and establish coherent thoughts helps them begin to understand. From time to time, you will need to know how things are going. Since understanding is an in-the-head matter, you will have to collect evidence about its quality from the children's responses and the ways in which they use their new-found understanding. But that is not the end of it. To stop there leaves this understanding to fend for itself too soon. It needs to be used, talked about, explored and developed.

Talk in any subject is demanding and not just for the child. To begin with, you may find that you have to give talk skills conscious thought as you use them. But, as when driving a car, the skills can become quite automatic and natural. As this begins to happen, you will be able to use them more flexibly and more effectively.

This book has been largely about creating and using opportunities for talk. Opportunities may be found anywhere but those that make the children want to explain, want to discuss and want to try out ideas are priceless, as is a touch of enthusiasm. You know your class better than anyone else so you are in the best position to judge what to try first. Whatever it is, do try it and do persist so that the children develop the habit of talking about their science and seeking an understanding.

Some possible responses to the tasks

For most tasks, several appropriate responses are possible. Some possible responses are suggested here but you may have ideas that suit your circumstances better. Just because your idea is not described does not mean it is necessarily inappropriate. The only true test of how good a teaching idea is, is to try it in your classroom. If it works, fine; if not, try another.

Introduction

Your science lessons

The questions do not cover everything about a lesson but are intended to give you a flavour of what the book is about. You may find it useful to revisit these questions to see if your interpretation has changed after you have read the book and tried out the ideas.

1.2 Some kinds of understanding in science

Facts, figures and understandings

Some examples from everyday life are given and (in parentheses) some examples are added from science.

Facts John has a car. (In science: some insects have wing cases.)

Figures It takes 20 minutes to get to school. (In science: an insect has six legs.)

Descriptive understanding John's car is a red hatchback with a dent in the driver's door. (In science: many birds tuck their legs in when flying.)

Explanatory understanding John had a crash because a tyre blew out. (In science: tucking legs in makes some birds more streamlined so they can fly with less effort.)

Descriptive procedural understanding To boil an egg, bring the water to the boil, adjust the heat so the water simmers, place the egg on a large spoon and lower it in the water, leave it to simmer for three and a half minutes . . . (In science: put the first shoe on the ramp, raise the ramp until the shoe just begins to slide, measure how high you had to raise the ramp, do it again for each shoe.)

Explanatory procedural understanding Put an egg cup on the bottle of milk so the birds cannot peck holes in the milk bottle top. (In science: put the first shoe on the ramp, raise the ramp until the shoe just begins to slide, measure how high you had to raise it, that tells you how much grip the shoe has on the ramp because the higher the ramp, the more grip there must be to prevent the shoe slipping.)

Facts, figures and understandings in science

The names of the planets Learning the names of planets does not involve a scientific understanding, the names are merely labels.

An eclipse You would probably want an explanatory understanding of an eclipse.

Where the wisdom teeth are The location of the wisdom teeth could involve a descriptive understanding but, if you went on to describe their function in relation to their location, it could include something of an explanatory understanding (for example, sharp-edged cutting teeth are at the front where they can bite off pieces of food; big, flat teeth for grinding food to a pulp are at the back where we chew; the wisdom teeth are chewing teeth and so are with the other chewing teeth.)

Elasticity Elasticity would involve at least a descriptive understanding of what the term means.

The life cycle of a butterfly The life cycle of a butterfly would involve at least a descriptive understanding. If, however, you explained pupation as a way of surviving the winter, that could amount to some explanatory understanding.

Separating a mixture of a soluble and an insoluble substance
Separating materials would involve descriptive procedural understanding

if no reasons for the procedure were included but explanatory procedural understanding if they were.

Testing the idea that running water can cause soil to be eroded   This can provide an understanding of soil erosion. That is, it offers an explanatory understanding if the children notice the fragments of soil being carried away by the water, if they also notice that the amount of soil remaining is decreasing, and if they tie the two together (the first being the cause of the second).

Sorting objects into metals and other materials   Successfully sorting materials into metals and non-metals by appearance could be based on a descriptive understanding.

Focusing on understandings

Some possibilities follow but you may have thought of others.

The naming of parts   The naming of parts would not, in itself, amount to an explanatory understanding but there could be a descriptive understanding associated with the appearance of the plant.

Testing threads   A descriptive procedural understanding would probably be involved unless the children could give reasons for the procedure, then it would become an explanatory procedural understanding.

Change   The distinction between melting and dissolving could be at the descriptive level of understanding. If, however, reference is made to the different behaviour of the tiny particles in the materials, this could amount to an explanatory understanding.

Forces   The children's suggestion that the number of wheels matters reflects their explanatory understanding. The experimental test led to its rejection. Subsequent exploration provided a descriptive understanding of what happens when more cars are added. If the children linked the effect with the greater inherent difficulty of moving larger masses, they would have established a better founded explanatory understanding.

Energy   The lesson began with some recall from an earlier lesson which may or may not involve understanding. Nevertheless, the children can explain, in terms of the rate of supply of materials in the blood, why their hearts beat faster if they run upstairs. This probably amounts to a simple but acceptable explanatory understanding at this stage. The subsequent experiments could involve explanatory procedural understanding if the children can justify and give reasons for the design of their investigations.

1.3 Getting to know the understandings you will support

Getting to know the understandings in a topic

Some possibilities are as follows.

Care for the environment Understand the concept of an environment. Understand why some environments need care.

Comparing people with other animals Understand the concept of an animal. Understand that humans are animals because of the biological features they have in common with other living things classed as animals.

Germs and healthy living Understand why dirty hands could lead to upset stomachs.

Loudness of sound Understand why loud sounds can damage hearing.

Musical instruments Understand the relationship between pitch and rate of vibration.

Pollution Understand the concept of pollution. Understand the causes of pollution.

Shadows Understand that shadows are caused by the obstruction of light from a light source.

Skeletons Understand why we have a skeleton.

Solids, liquids and gases Understand the concepts of solid, liquid and gas.

The scientist Understand the concept of a scientist. Understand why the scientist investigates with fair tests.

The seasons   Understand what makes the seasons.

Transparency   Understand the concept of being transparent and being opaque.

1.4 Scientific language

Being familiar

Science may be expressed in simple, familiar terms in several ways and what is familiar and simple to one child may not be to another. You will know better than most what is more likely to be meaningful to the children you teach. Remember that simple, familiar terms may not express the science as precisely as the scientific expression but they are starting points from which the appropriate vocabulary may be developed.

Sound   Things that shake or shiver may make a sound we can hear. A better word is *vibrate*. Things that vibrate may make a sound we can hear. A sound can bounce around a large, empty room. Sound does not bounce off curtains and carpets half as well as it bounces off walls. Curtains and carpets absorb some of the sound and so make a room quieter.

Friction   Friction pulls back on things. Some liquids are a bit like treacle and do not run quickly because of the friction between the little bits of treacle. Oil smoothes over the rough bits so there is less friction.

Space   The earth turns like this [demonstrate with a globe]. See how it turns on this axle? The earth does not have an axle through it but where it would go is called the earth's *axis*. The earth turns on its axis. We say that the earth *rotates* on its axis. The moon goes around the earth like this [demonstrates]. We say it *revolves* around the earth. The earth *revolves* around the sun. The sun rotates on its own axis, just like the earth. There is next to nothing out there between the planets. When there is nothing at all, absolutely nothing, we call it a *vacuum*.

Life   What is the same about all these plants? All of them have green bits, don't they? The green stuff in these plants, with the help of sunlight, makes some of the things the plants need to live. We cannot use sunlight like this ourselves because we do not have what it takes in our skin. We are not plants. There are very, very, tiny living things which are so small you cannot see them unless you have a really powerful magnifier. We call them *microbes*. Think about where you live, eat and shop. Living things need somewhere to live. They have to be able to eat, survive and have young. They need a place where they can do all that. We call a place like that a *habitat*. What is a worm's habitat? What about a rabbit?

Making meaning

A fair test   A possible starting point would be to describe an event that was not fair. For example, a 100 m race where one person started half way along the track, another had to wait 5 seconds after the rest had started, and another had both feet tied together. 'Does it tell you who is the best runner?' 'Why not?' 'How can we put it right?' Key words and phrases might be: fair, unfair, making things the same, having an equal chance.

Care for the environment   One way to begin would be to introduce something concrete and meaningful to think with. 'How many people are there in this school?' 'How many are in this town?' 'What if everyone dropped a plastic cup like this every day for a year? How many cups would there be lying around?' 'People throw out more than this. How much do they throw away each week?' 'What would it be like living among all this?' 'What about other living things, the animals and plants? What would they find difficult about it?' Key words and phrases might be: surroundings, mess, litter, pollution.

Characteristics of living things   This might begin with *Ourselves* and then look for similarities with other animals. Initially, this would focus on physical characteristics and then develop into a comparison of basic behaviours, such as eating, sleeping, moving and excreting. Key words and phrases might be: just like us, what we all have, what we all look like, what we all do.

A gas   The most familiar 'gas' for children may be that which is used to heat houses. Its nature might be explored. 'Can you smell it?' 'What's it look like?' The concept needs to be widened to include air and other gases. 'Have you seen the bubbles that you get in pop? What are they?' 'This is another kind of gas. It's not like the gas used for central heating. How is it different?' 'How is it the same?' You may be able to show the children a silvered balloon that has another gas in it that is so light it makes the balloon float (hydrogen or helium). You could contrast it with one that falls to the floor because it is filled with air. Now you have introduced air, the children can explore it directly but you may need to remember that air and household gas are both mixtures of gases. You may find it productive to have the children compare gases with liquids and solids.

2.1 Guiding thought

Planning your own tuning-talk

Not all stones are the same   For example, 'Have you ever looked closely at the pebbles on the beach?' 'Did you see them building a new wall today?' 'Were they using bricks?' 'What was it they were using instead of bricks?'

Soils   For example, 'What is under your feet?' 'And what is under that?' 'And what is under that?' 'Is there soil under everything?' 'How deep is soil?' 'Is it all the same?'

Planning your own connecting-talk

'What are those little bits, Miss?'   You might show the children dust on a shelf and blow it off, making the tiny bits more visible with torch-light. 'Is it like what we saw in the sunlight?'

Food chains   You might begin with what the children eat and then talk about familiar food chains, such as birds–worms–leaves, before moving to less familiar food chains. 'What's the same about all of these?' 'What do they all start with?' 'What do they all end with?'

Planning your own monitoring-talk

Day and night   For example, 'Why is it so dull when it's very cloudy?' 'Why is it dark at night?'

The cause of shadows   For example, 'What happens to shadows when it is very cloudy?' and 'Why do you think that is?'; 'Look, I'm going to shine the torch on Teddy. Where will Teddy's shadow be?' and 'Why?'

Sources of light and reflectors of light   For example, 'Oh, dear! I have to look in my dark cupboard. There are no windows and the light won't work. I haven't got a torch. What can I do? Will this help me see?' [showing a mirror].

The life cycle of a frog   For example, 'Tell me what you think it will look like when it's half way between a tadpole and a frog.' 'When it becomes a frog, what happens next?' 'Why do you think we call it a cycle?'

The process of condensation   For example, 'Look, see what's running down the window. Where did the water come from?' 'If I breathed on a warm piece of glass, would it be different?' and 'Why?'

Checking that erosion is not confused with weathering   For example, using pictures of erosion and weathering, 'Look at this picture. What made this happen?' 'What do we call that?'

2.2   Science talk and practical activity

Using talk to support practical activity

What is soil?   In the first section: the teacher might ask questions that elicit prior knowledge, such as, 'What is soil?' 'Where does it come from?' 'Does it all look the same?' 'Does it all feel the same?' In the second section: for example, 'What have you found out?' 'Show me how you know that.' 'What would happen if . . .' In the third section: for example, 'Why does it settle in layers?' In the last section: for example, 'Why do you think that sand, pebbles and some humus make a kind of soil?'

Can we make clay drain better?   In the first section: the teacher might ask questions that elicit prior knowledge, such as 'What things let water through easily?' 'What things do not let water through easily?' 'What is the difference between the two?' In the second section: for example, 'Tell me what is different about the soils.' 'How does that make this one drain better?' 'What would happen if we squashed this soil? Would it drain better?' 'What makes you think that?' In the third section: for example, 'Which one do you think will drain better?' 'Why do you think that?' 'Tell me why doing that makes it a good test.' In the last section: 'So you would ask the farmer to mix some sand with his clay soil?' 'Why will that make it better?' 'I know that the farmer will not want to go to all that hard work and expense without being fairly sure that it will work. How will you convince him to give it a try? What will you say?' 'How will that convince him?'

Practically talking

Developing the children's experience – absorbency The children could be given sponges, wipes and kitchen paper to examine with a hand lens. Before they use them, you could ask them to describe these objects and compare their appearance. You might then have them dip one corner of each object into water and watch the water soak into the material. You could ask them to explain why some soak up water better than others.

A more prescriptive activity – how fast does grass grow? You could have the children grow grass from grass seed in compost in pots. Once established, they could measure its growth regularly. You could ask if it grows the same amount every day. If not, why not? What makes grass grow better on some days than on others?

An investigation – the most squashy thing I can find The children should have explored the property of squashiness earlier and arrived at a possible cause. This should allow them to choose likely candidates and predict which will be the most squashy. You could, for instance, ask why they think that object will be more squashy than the other ones. How will they know if their prediction is wrong? What will that tell them about their idea about what makes things squashy?

Developing the children's experience – erosion The children could observe how water from a watering can erode a heap of soil. You might ask where the soil is going. Where has the mud come from? What bits are left behind? What shapes does the water make? What will happen, eventually?

A more prescriptive activity – can plants in the shade do anything about it? You could place one small bean plant behind a relatively small screen and leave another in full light. The children could draw the plants each day to form a sequence of small pictures that show the growth patterns of the two plants. The children can staple these sets of pictures together to make 'movies' of the growth by flicking through them. 'What is different about the one behind the screen?' 'What seems to be attracting it?' 'If we left it long enough, what would happen?'

An investigation – does water evaporate more quickly if you spread it out? The children can probably construct a reason for why pools having equal amounts of water should evaporate at different rates if they have different surface areas. 'Which one do you think will dry up first?' 'Why do you think that?' 'How can we test your idea?'

Monitoring-talk to gauge an understanding of an investigation

Snow time For example, 'What are we trying to find out?' 'Would it be right if we used a big snowball and a little snowball?' 'Why do you think that?' 'What have we found out?' 'How do you know that?'

The best wash For example, 'So, what exactly are we trying to find out?' 'How will we know which one is the best?' 'What do we mean by "best"?'

2.3 Changing minds

Using talk to help change minds

Too much or too little discrimination

- *Excluding people and minibeasts (e.g. insects) from the animal world*: the child probably thinks of 'people' as a special or unique category of its own. In everyday conversation, we generally do not call minibeasts, such as insects, animals. Again, they are probably considered to be in a class of their own although this class may have rather vague boundaries. Discussing what these animals do have in common with other animals is a starting point.
- *Excluding trees from plants*: woody plants often seem so different from soft stemmed, herbaceous plants that their common features may be overlooked. Again, discussing what they have in common is a starting point.
- *Wild animals are dangerous*: presenting the child with contrary instances is a starting point. (Have you ever been eaten by a slow worm or beaten up by a squirrel?)

- *Materials* tends to refer to fabrics in everyday usage. Explaining to children that the word covers a wider range of things is a start. Having them identify different materials using a key helps to establish the concept. (The dual usage of this term may be readily appreciated by children and so could be a useful examplar that shows the distinction between scientific and everyday language.)
- *Dissolving or melting?* These two processes are sometimes confused by children because the end point is a liquid in both cases and many adults do not distinguish clearly between them. First-hand experience, careful observation, description and discussion about the differences are starting points.

Views of how the world works

- *Bodies like cucumbers*: you can begin to change this idea if you have a transparent model of the human body to talk about. Otherwise, a picture that shows its inner structure can be useful.
- *The world is flat*: to a child, this is obvious: their eyes confirm it. Adjusting their ideas takes time. Pictures of the earth from space shuttles provides food for thought – and talk.
- *The sun moves across the sky*: like the flat earth, this is what your eyes tell you. It is another example of how common sense can lead thoughts astray. Models of the solar system help but the children need to appreciate that it is possible to believe that something is moving when, in fact, it is they who are moving. For instance, you might talk about how the scenery seems to rush past the moving car or train window.
- *Light is emitted from the eyes*: some children may think that vision entails the emission of something from the eyes (something that is reinforced by the fictional beings who can 'look' at something and can see its interior with their 'X-ray vision'). Alternatively, children may confuse the direction of a look with the path that the light takes. The first idea could be discussed in the context of what they would 'see' inside a windowless cupboard with the door closed. The second needs a careful distinction drawn between looking and seeing.
- *Weight increases with height*: this possibly comes from the common experience that it seems more tiring to hold something at arm's length than it is to let your hand hang down by your side. The children can test their idea using a force meter or a set of scales, discussing the meaning of what they find.

2.4 Pressing for understanding

Hard pressed

Shadows *Tuning-talk*: for example, 'It's a hot day today. If you want to keep cool, where's the best place in the playground?' 'Why's that a good place?' *Connecting-talk*: for example, 'So why is it dark on that side of the wall?' 'Why is it not dark on the other side?' *Monitoring-talk*: for example, 'If I hold Teddy up, where will the shadow be?' 'How will we know it's Teddy's shadow?'

Health *Tuning-talk*: for example, 'I'll bet you've been told to go and play in the fresh air. Why's fresh air good for you?' 'What is air like that isn't fresh?' 'Why might it be bad for you?' *Connecting-talk*: for example, 'Why might smoking be bad for you?' *Monitoring-talk*: for example, 'Some people chew tobacco. What do you think of that?'

3.1 Building bridges

Constructing a bridge

Being healthy You could make an analogy with a mechanical toy, highlighting the difference between working and broken. This is limited, however, to the obvious mechanical failure of the human body, as when there are broken bones. You would need to extend it by reference to the children's own experiences of infection and the invisible world that causes it.

Life cycles The essential concept here is 'cycle' and the repetition that it implies. Examples of obvious repeating sequences could be used to introduce this pattern of nature. There are, for instance, the meals of the day, day and night, and the seasons. In the children's own lives, they will see babies become adults who, in turn, have babies.

Animal skeletons Analogies with a cage (the ribs), a crash helmet (the skull) and tubes (the long bones) will draw attention to the structural function of the skeleton.

Friction between two solid surfaces You might, for instance, begin with friction between two sheets of sandpaper and compare it with the friction felt between two sheets of brown paper. The children can see and feel the surfaces and compare them. The next step could be to examine a variety of surfaces with a hand lens and predict what it would be like if one was rubbed on another.

Conduction of heat   Generally, the aim is that the children should learn that heat is transmitted through solid objects, some better than others. The 'bits' of the material vibrate when heated and pass these vibrations on to other 'bits'. Eventually, the vibrations reach the parts farthest from the heat source and are passed on to our hands: a sensation we call heat. This invisible process can be made visible using the children themselves to make an analogy. They form a line, all facing one way, with hands on the shoulders of the person in front, keeping arms relatively stiff (like the 'bits' in the object). The one at the 'hot' end of the line is made to vibrate relatively slowly. The vibrations will be passed down the line to the other end.

3.2   Science talk and scaffolding

Scaffolding children's thinking

Sorting leaves   A starting point is to check that the child knows what he or she is supposed to be doing. You could then take a leaf and draw attention to some obvious characteristics (for example, finger-like edges/ no finger-like edges). You could ask the child to find another leaf that was like this one and start a pile for the child who then proceeds with the sorting. Afterwards, you would probably return and ask about other characteristics (for example, hairy/smooth leaves) and the child sorts leaves according to this characteristic. This time, you do not start the pile for the child but wait for him or her to begin.

Mice keeping warm   It may be that the children have not grasped the point of the exercise. Refer to their own experiences and break the problem down into small units. How do they keep warm on a cold day? Does the mouse have a thick coat to put on? Does it need a thick coat? The next part is to do with food. How do they get food? Can the mouse go to the shop? Finally, turn their attention to how the mouse is equipped to detect predators. At each stage, try to give a little less help. (A story to go with this is Eric Carle's *The Mixed Up Chameleon*, published by Penguin, London, 1988, in which a chameleon tries out the shape and form of other animals but finds them unsuited to its needs. See also '3.6 Science talk and stories', pp. 95–101.)

Lagging the water tank   You would probably check first that the child grasped the purpose of the investigation. Next, you might ask how he or she keeps warm. What materials are best for keeping warm? Which materials are less good? Why? Then have the child predict which will be best and worst among those materials that are available. How can we find out if we are right? Encourage the child to show you how he or she will make a fair test. You might also ask what measurements will be taken and how these will provide the information needed to decide which material is best.

Sources of light   You may feel you should check that the children do grasp that a source of light produces light itself and does not merely reflect it. To see if the children really do believe that a reflector, such as a piece of foil, produces light itself you could ask them to describe what it would be like in a dark cave if they took a piece of foil out of a bag. Some children may see it as a matter of degree. The foil would illuminate the cave but not as well as a torch. That is, the foil is a weaker source of light than a torch. One approach would be to place reflectors and sources of light in a box that has a tiny peep hole and is in a relatively dark room. You describe and explain what you see and the child takes a turn. A new object is placed inside the box and the process is repeated, this time allowing the child to take the lead.

3.3   Science talk and modelling thinking

Modelling your thinking for the children

Squashed: making sense of data   For example: some of the things were squashed more than the others. All the bricks that stand on them are the same so this sponge must be the most squashy and the cardboard squares the least squashy. The carpet pieces are a bit squashy, more than the cardboard but not as much as the sponge.

Mopping up: making sense of data   For example: the first one soaked up 17 drops. That's the least of all. The last one soaked up most, 61 drops. Why's that? It's furry. The second one is furry, too. It held a fair amount of water. It looks like being furry helps things soak up water. Wait a minute. Let's put them in order. Smooth with few holes first; smooth and lots of holes second; furry, few holes third; furry, lots of holes, most. Yes, it looks like furry helps quite a bit. Lots of holes helps a bit, too. To help the children join in, you might pause at some point: 'Now what? I wonder. Any ideas? Can you help me out?'

3.4 Science talk and predicting

Helping children make predictions

The best hat You might begin by discussing what, in general, keeps the sun off us. Does a window? Does an umbrella? Is an umbrella better than a postage stamp? When the children predict which hat is the best, you should have them justify their choice.

Overcooked biscuits You may, for example, show loaves of bread that have been baked to different degrees. You could ask the children to tell you about what happens to toast if it is left too long in the toaster. Then you could move on to biscuits and have them predict what will happen. They should, of course, give a reason to underpin the prediction.

Tomorrow's poppy Poppies drop their petals quickly so they will have to be fresh to begin with. You might begin by asking what generally happens to flowers. You may take the opportunity to use more precise terms to help them describe what happens, such as wilt, petal, seed head. On this basis, they can predict what will happen, with good reason, and see it occur almost before their eyes.

The best parachute What makes things float in the air? What about dandelion seeds? How do people in aeroplanes escape? What are parachutes like? What makes a good parachute? Why do you think that?

The fastest boat The pattern could be like that described for the parachute. You could begin with fish and submarine shapes.

The hardest rock Direct experience with a variety of rocks, feeling them and examining them with magnifiers, is a starting point. The children can use this to predict which they think is the hardest and describe what they think makes it the hardest.

Monitoring understanding through prediction

Head to head A first step could be to ask for the reasons for the responses. Underneath both of them might lie an understanding that could be developed. For instance, the child who says, 'Blow up', may think the batteries will pump electricity into one another until they reach the limits of their capacity and then burst like a balloon. The one who says, 'Nothing', may see the batteries as attempting to push electricity into one another but, as they are equally matched, neither can overcome the other. The next step would probably be to try it. At least one of these children will need to reconsider the thinking behind his or her suggestion.

3.5   Science talk and inanimate teachers

Talk and inanimate teachers

This depends, of course, on what you choose and what you want it to do. Suppose it was a videotape. In general, you could begin *before* starting the player by asking the children what they think the videotape will be about. An alternative for older children is to provide three key words about the topic and ask the children for others that they associate with them. You can, of course, also ask for the basis of each association. You could state the learning goals of the session as this tends to focus attention on information relating to these. Again, with older children, you could talk through a diagram that shows the structure of the presentation. *During* the presentation, you might stop the tape at the end of a unit and ask the children to tell you what they think the most important points are. Alternatively, they could explain what they have seen or draw a diagram to summarize it. *After* the video, you might ask for an oral summary or work with the children to construct a graphic organizer that captures the main features of the presentation. You could also take it further by asking for applications of their understanding and explanations of matters they did not see in the video-taught session.

3.6   Science talk and stories

Teacher talk and stories

Thomas the Tiger Keeps Cool You might include in the tuning-talk questions about how the children feel and what they do to keep cool on really hot days. A pause for connecting-talk might occur, for example, after 'But the river was not in the forest. There were no trees on the river bank.' You might ask, 'Why is shade nice on a hot day?' 'What things make it shady? How do they make it shady? What happens to all the heat that can't get at you?' At the end of the story, you might explore the ideas practically with the children. 'Where would it be coolest in the playground?' 'Why do you think it would be cool there?' 'What about that place?' 'Why do you think that would be warm?' 'Let's see if you are right. We'll stand in both places and try it.' In effect, your monitoring-talk asks the children to apply their ideas.

The Very Dirty Giant Your tuning-talk might include some questions about having an upset stomach, its possible causes and the need for hygiene. A pause for connecting-talk could occur after, for example, the paragraph describing the giant sneezing and the fly settling on the shovelful of pie. You might ask the children to explain why these could spread diseases. Monitoring-talk could solicit other 'at-risk' situations from the children.

3.7 Science talk and games

Game time

Living, once-living, never lived For example, you might invent a game of Snap with a range of pictures on the cards. 'Snap' constitutes a justified match of living, once-living, never lived. In effect, the children have to apply their understanding of these concepts. So, for instance, a picture of a wooden toy followed by a picture of a book is an opportunity for a Snap as both are examples of 'once-living' (trees).

Changes For example, this might be achieved with a card game where the pack comprises before changes, after changes and reasons. It might be played by one person by setting the cards out as you would for a game of Patience. In effect, the child has to make the connections. An example would be pictures of wheat (before change) and bread (after change). This is a permanent change brought about by heat.

Camouflage For example, this might comprise a large, complex picture with hidden animals. Points are awarded for finding the animals. 'Why is it hard to find them?' is one question that might follow.

The right one for the job   For example, this could be another card game of Snap where the aim is to notice cards that match the 'job' and the material (for instance, a picture of a wall and a picture of brick clay). It could also be a game where the aim is to 'collect' materials that will complete a task or solve a problem, such as building a house (materials for the roof, window, door, floor, wall and foundations).

These are merely suggestions; many games are possible.

3.8   Science talk and graphic organizers

Graphically organized

This depends on what it is you choose to show. Some possibilities are as follows.

The things that plants need to grow   You would probably want to depict at least water (perhaps as rain), light (probably from the sun) and the plant with its roots in a source of nutrients (probably soil).

Squashing, bending, twisting and stretching   You may want to illustrate permanent and temporary physical changes, you could have a circle for each of these kinds of force. Each circle could be subdivided into two, one for those materials that show temporary change and one for those that show permanent change.

Choosing the right material for the job   You could depict a house with arrows pointing to the roof, walls, gutters, windows, curtains and paths. At the end of each arrow would be the property that is appropriate for those materials with a space for a brief justification.

Cool in summer – warm in winter   This could be shown by two pictures, side by side, one of a child dressed for a hot day in summer and one dressed for a cold day in winter. The aim would be to have the children compare the materials to identify what properties are likely to keep heat in (or let it out). Afterwards, they might test their ideas practically. If they do, another graphic organizer could be produced by discussion to depict the procedure they would follow.

Solids, liquids and gases   An organizer could comprise ruled lines to make three vertical columns, one for each state. A diagrammatic representation of a solid, liquid and gas could be at the top of each column and an explanation added under each diagram.

Natural and manufactured materials   An organizer could be two columns used to list such materials with a justification of the lists.

Activity pictures

This depends on what you choose. Some possibilities are the following.

Not all flowers are the same   You might structure the inquiry so that the children compare flowers in a systematic way. By discussion, you could agree to begin with, say, the flower (colour, number of petals, shape of petal), leaf (shape, edges, distribution along the stem), stem (shape of cross-section). Each step could be shown in a flow chart.

How fast does grass grow?   An organizer could be a table for day by day recording of the length of grass growing in a pot.

Taking the sand out of some sandy water by filtering   This could be a flow chart representing the filtering sequence. It is easy for such flow charts to become instructions to follow without understanding so you may arrive at them by discussion and press for the reasons that underpin them.

What is it that makes a good oven glove?   Things to investigate could be the material's size, thickness, material and colour. These might be set out like the fading of sugar paper activity in Figure 3.6 (see p. 109).

What is it that makes some stones 'skip' over water?   Some possibilities are thickness, material, speed of throw and angle of throw relative to the surface of the water. As above, these might be set out as in Figure 3.6.

Pictorial analogies

This depends on what you choose but, to be effective, the analogy needs to be based on something that the children already know well (or something you are prepared to teach them about first).

The strength of leg bones   A common analogy is to relate the leg bones to the metal tubes used for table legs and chair legs.

Solids, liquids and gases   An analogy for the distinction between these three states may be made using the children themselves. When they all hold hands, their movement is limited (the solid). It is greater when they are broken into smaller groups (the liquid). They can move around most easily when they are all free (the gas). Note, however, in the case of a material, it is usually the application of heat that shakes the bits about enough to break up the hand-holding.

Sound travelling through air One analogy is to line up dominoes to represent slices of air. When you push over the end one (like a shout in air), a chain reaction begins which passes down the line to the other end (where the ear would be). A slinky spring shows the effect better as it can move to and fro continuously, rather like what happens in the air. The dominoes, of course, fall only in one direction and so lack this to and fro motion.

4.2 Conversations from events

Seizing the moment

The hole in the ground involves an event that could be a starting point for a conversation about 'what it is like under our feet', soil, subsoil and on to the centre of the earth. The refuse problem may introduce a conversation relating to health hazards. Some children think that the reason they should avoid refuse is because it smells and is dirty. Quite what 'dirty' means tends to be vague. We tend to take drainage for granted until the drains block. What happens to the water that goes through the drains? Where does it go? The flowers are all very different. Are bought flowers different from wild flowers? Wet leaves on the road can be a greater danger. The conversation might try to identify why leaves can be a problem in autumn. The hot air balloon just floats in the air. How can it hold up that large basket with a person in it?

4.3 Conversations from children's questions

Engaging conversations

I wonder How does a grasshopper make a noise? Their back legs are a bit like combs. Rubbing them together makes a noise like when you drag a comb across the edge of the table. A raindrop falling goes faster and faster with the air whizzing past. Eventually, it can go no faster then . . . splat! The aim is for the children to imagine themselves running down the hill, going faster and faster. They then meet another hill and their momentum will carry them part of the way up it. After that, they will run backwards, and so on. The children must imagine themselves subject to the force of gravity and 'free-wheeling', that is, adding no force of their own. The intention is for the children to draw on their own experience and relate it to what happens to the car.

Some electrifying questions   One approach would be to take these in reverse order, beginning with why the word 'volts' appears on the battery. You could have one group of children (including the one whose question it is) research that problem by looking in books. They will probably find out about Allessandro Volta, the Italian scientist who made and investigated simple batteries. At the same time, they should find some information to report back that is relevant to the next question, 'What is inside a battery?' This leads naturally into the report of another group who researched the structure of modern batteries. The last question, to do with why electricity does not run out of a battery, is one for another group, with contributions from everyone.

4.4   Conversations from artefacts

Artefacts as conversation pieces

There are many ways of interpreting such artefacts. Here are just a few ways of initiating and maintaining a conversation. In practice, you should be prepared to follow potentially useful directions that the children take themselves.

A freshly cut log   Is it a plant? Is it living, once living or dead? What are the rings at the ends? Which part is the hardest? For comparison, you could have a length of raw timber to show that the wood we use in the home is the same as that in this log. What will happen to the log if it is left outside? Would this happen to the length of timber? How do we stop it from happening?

A fruit   What are they? What are they like inside? Are all fruits like this? What happens to them if no one eats them? A jar of fruit can be a useful addition.

A spider   You may have been teaching about minibeasts, what they are and how they live. Perhaps you have introduced the use of simple identification keys. You are about to conclude the topic when you spot this truly enormous spider in the entrance to the school. You capture it in a transparent container. 'Look what I've found!' you announce with enthusiasm. The children are curious and nervous.

A hard hat   The children often know what a hard hat is but they are sometimes surprised to find that it is often made from a plastic. Objects with a similar function are the human skull, domes on buildings and even egg shells.

4.5   Conversations from pictures

Talking pictures

As when using artefacts, pictures may offer a number of possibilities. A few are illustrated here. Again, you should be prepared to follow potentially useful paths that the children take.

Dinosaur picture   You might begin with an exploration of the picture. 'What's this picture about?' 'How big would this one be?' 'As big as the school?' 'Are there animals like this alive today?' The next step could be to interpret the picture. For example, you might ask: 'What do you think this one eats?' 'Why do you think that?' 'I wonder which one moves the fastest?' 'What makes you think that?' Then you might open it up: 'I wonder why there are no animals like this today.' 'What would it be like when dinosaurs were around.' 'What would it be like if there were dinosaurs today.' 'How do we know there were ever dinosaurs at all?'

Picture of the moon   Again, you might begin by exploring the picture. 'What is it?' 'What are these parts here?' 'Is there water on the moon?' 'What are craters?' Then you might open it up: 'What made these craters?' 'I wonder why the earth isn't covered in craters like the moon?' 'Are there any craters on the earth? I think I'll look at the map of the world. Just a minute, I've got this picture of a crater on the Earth here.' 'I wonder what it would be like to live on the moon.' 'What would we have to take with us?' 'You know that a few people have been to the moon but have you ever seen pictures of their footprints? They look as though they'll last forever. What do you think?' 'Why's that?'

Conversations from stories and poems

Telling tales

No Lollipop Today The story illustrates the way some colours are more easily seen than others. Have the children ever experienced something similar themselves? Which car colours are easier to see? How can they make themselves visible on a bicycle or when crossing the road? Using a shoe box with a viewing hole in it and squares of different coloured paper inside, you could demonstrate that some colours are, indeed, easier to see in dim light than others. Have they any bright ideas for using colours that are easily seen?

The Flow of Blood This story describes the action of the heart and the function of blood and also puts the scientist back into the science. Some questions to stimulate talk could be: what are the blue lines we can sometimes see under our skin? What can blood do? What happens when you cut yourself? Why does it clot? Why do hospitals need blood? Is everyone's blood exactly the same? What is blood pressure? There are many things to talk about once we begin to talk about ourselves.

4.7 Who takes the initiative?

Dealing with the unexpected

In all cases, you might say, 'Let's find a book about . . . and see if it tells us'. This has the virtue of helping the children practise their information finding skills. Should you choose to provide some information yourself, try to engage the child in discussion about it. Often, some of the things that children ask are worth exploring with the whole class; what puzzles or interests one is likely to puzzle or interest others. Here are a few suggestions for the instances listed.

Dinosaurs 'No one knows for sure. Some scientists think that a big meteor from space hit the earth and the dust and smoke blotted out the sun. Perhaps the dinosaurs died because there was nothing much to eat. Just think about it, what would it be like if it was dark all night *and* all day? What would happen to all the plants and what about the animals that eat them?'

Aliens 'I don't really know. Let's think about it like a detective. Is there any evidence?' 'Is it good evidence? Let's talk about it.'

Rainbows 'Do you remember how we made rainbows when we let sunlight go through those pieces of plastic? Well, raindrops are a bit like those pieces of plastic. They split up the light into its colours. I once made a rainbow with a spray of water drops from a hose when I was washing my car. Have you ever seen a rainbow made another way? Let's find out if there are any other ways'

Thorny question 'Well, you tell me. What do cows and sheep eat?' 'What if grasses had thorns on them?' 'So how does having thorns help some plants?' 'I wonder if thorns can help plants in other ways? Let's see if we can find out.'

Glossary

At times, you may dip into this book and want to be reminded of terms that were introduced earlier. This brief glossary is intended to help in that event.

Analogy A parallel drawn between something to be understood in science and something that is already known well to the learner.

Connecting-talk Classroom discourse with the primary intention of helping children make mental connections, structures and relationships and reasons to do with what is to be understood.

Discourse In the context of this book, this refers to the science talk that takes place in the classroom. Often, it is between the teacher and one or more children but it can be between children.

Focused talk and conversation Focused talk is verbal interaction that the teacher largely controls and directs towards specific ends, generally the support of specific kinds of learning. Tuning-talk, connecting-talk and monitoring-talk are examples. A conversation is less controlled but can support learning by exploring and exercising it and by providing opportunities for developing it. This use of a conversation recognizes the individual differences in learning that result from focused talk.

Graphic organizer A diagram or diagram-like depiction that organizes information to make relationships or patterns more noticeable.

Language in science Science has a specialist vocabulary that can make it difficult for a non-specialist to grasp. Some terms may be taken from everyday language but have a more precise or even different meaning in science. Language structures that are common in science may be less common in everyday language.

Memorization The committing of information to memory without understanding.

Modelling In this context, what the teacher does to illustrate how something may be done, particularly in the thinking processes.

Monitoring-talk Classroom discourse with the primary intention of assessing the quantity and quality of learning. It includes discourse intended to clarify the nature of a misunderstanding.

Press for understanding Teaching that demands that learners justify assertions and demonstrate their grasp of the purpose, structure, relationships and reasons involved in what they are learning.

Scaffolding Supporting a child's thinking by structuring the process and guiding the child through it. The support is progressively reduced until the child can perform independently.

Tuning-talk Classroom discourse aimed at activating relevant prior knowledge. It includes what is said to focus attention, make good or adjust prior knowledge, and motivate the child at the outset.

Understanding The kind of learning that involves knowing purposes, structures, relationships and reasons. There are many kinds of understanding. For example, when they enable a description of a situation, as in describing the relative location of the organs of the body, it is a descriptive understanding. When they enable an explanation, as in explaining why an event occurs, it is an explanatory understanding. When they involve knowing why a particular procedure is effective, it is a procedural understanding.

Further reading and some examples of resources to support science talk and conversations

Newton, D.P. (2000) *Teaching for Understanding: what it is and how to do it* (London, RoutledgeFalmer) describes the nature of understanding and ways of helping learners of all ages understand. It includes, for instance, how to use analogies, how to use text effectively, what happens when understanding fails, and what might be done about it. For those with responsibility for science in the primary school, you might find the following useful: Newton, L.D. and Newton, D.P. (1998) *Coordinating Science across the Primary School* (London, Falmer). For those setting out to teach science, you could try: Newton, L.D. (2000) *Meeting the Standards in Primary Science* (London, RoutledgeFalmer). This describes much of what is involved in becoming a competent teacher of science in the primary school. For those with a general interest in the nature of science, Wolpert, L. (1993) *The Unnatural Nature of Science* (London, Faber and Faber) is a very readable book about the way common sense can mislead and how what we need is uncommon sense in science.

A book describing research in the USA on science talk, highlighting its importance is by Lemke, J.L. (1990) *Talking Science* (Norwood, New Jersey, Ablex). One that offers some views on the language of science, how it differs from the vernacular and the possible significance of the differences for teaching is by Halliday, M.A.K. and Martin, J.R. (1993) *Writing Science* (London, Falmer). The following may be useful for those who wish to study classroom talk in research settings. Edwards, A.D. and Westgate, D.P.G. (1987) *Investigating Classroom Talk* (London, Falmer).

Some books about using stories and poems to support understanding in science are: Association for Science Education (2000) *Science, Technology and Reading: a resource for teachers* (Hatfield, Herts, Association of Science Education). This illustrates the use of poems to introduce a variety of scientific ideas. After each poem, it provides discussion points, some scientific background and some activities. Parr, B. and Graham, M. (1995) *Science from Rhymes* (London, Questions/Watts) is similar in aim to the preceding book and is better suited to younger learners. Ellis, B. (1997) *Learning from the Land* (Englewood, Colorado, Teacher Ideas Press) is a book about using stories to set the scene for activities to do with ecology. Lipke, B. (1996) *Figures, Facts and Fables: telling tales in science and math* (Heinemann, Portsmouth, New Hampshire) describes how children can tell their own stories to describe the science they do. A useful point that Lipke makes is that less able children find this an easier way of expressing their thoughts. Note, however, that some educators argue that having children tell stories like this (as opposed to a teacher using a story as an instrument for supporting learning) is not doing science, see Halliday and Martin, above. It could be argued, of course, that this device is a more or less temporary bridge that helps children into science. Naylor, B. and Naylor, S. (2000) *The Seesaw and Other Science Questions* (London, Hodder Children's Books) is an example of a book from a series. Each sets a scene, asks questions and suggests investigations. Books of this nature lend themselves to supporting science talk and conversations. Gaynor, B. (1997) *What Keeps Them Warm* (Walton-on-Thames, Surrey, Thomas Nelson) is one book in a series available in Big Book format. This format lends itself to supporting science talk with young children. Chancellor, D. (ed.) (1993) *The Dorling Kindersley Picturepedia* (London, Dorling Kindersley) is, in essence, a book of annotated pictures and is a source of illustrations that may be used to stimulate conversations in science.

There are other materials with the potential to be useful or which offer useful advice. For example, Glower, D. (1997) *Science Dictionary* (Oxford, Heinemann Educational) is a tool for developing scientific vocabulary but, of course, the words have to be given meaning and talk can help to do that. Tarquin, P. and Walker, S. (1996) *Creating Success in the Classroom* (Englewood, Colorado, Teacher Ideas Press) describes a wide range of graphical organizers and how to use them in the classroom. A short book that offers a number of ideas for supporting practical work in science, one of which is the Concept Cartoon (described as a kind of graphic organizer in section 3.8) is by Keogh, B. and Naylor S. (1997) *Starting Points for Science* (Sandbach, Millgate House).

Some useful advice relevant to initiating and maintaining conversations in science may be found in Department for Education and Employment (1999) *National Literacy Strategy Leaflets* (London, The Stationery Office). *Talking in Class (No. 1), Engaging all Pupils (No. 2)* and *Looking for Patterns (No. 3)* are particularly relevant.

General index

This index deals with the educational ideas that underly the use of talk to support understanding in science. For specific teaching ideas, see the Science topic index that follows.

Science topic index

This index lists the content by science-related topic so that specific teaching ideas and considerations may be located more readily.